PRAISE

" *If you can read only one book on diversity and inclusion, it should be* Women, Minorities, & Other Extraordinary People. *Barbara Adams leaves no doubt about the destructiveness of discrimination and proposes creative, workable approaches to the difficult task of building and retaining a diverse, inclusive workforce. She compels readers to recognize and understand the urgency of dealing with hidden biases and corrects deep-rooted misconceptions that create impediments to a desirable work environment. This book offers a practical road map for reframing the thinking required to embrace the diversity and inclusion that make companies and organizations more successful. It is a must-read!*"

—Ambassador Ruth A. Davis (Ret.),
named to *The Economist's* 2015 Global Diversity List
as one of the Top 50 Diversity Figures in Public Life

" *For as much as we talk about diversity and inclusion in the workplace, it is so misunderstood. What's distinct about this book is the depth of conversation and action it can inspire.*"

—Bärí A. Williams, tech industry legal and operations executive,
start-up advisor, former lead counsel for Facebook,
creator of Facebook's Supplier Diversity Program

" *Dr. Adams compassionately 'cracks the code' for how to achieve inclusion through diversity as both business and moral imperative. Her book is a must-read for anyone who wants to make a positive difference and move the needle in the right direction toward rebuilding organizations that are equitable and inclusive. Through her masterful storytelling and impeccable research, Dr. Adams helps you to understand why it's important that* everyone *in your organization must be made to feel like they belong and belong uniquely."*

—Demetriouse Russell, founder at
Venn Diagram Partners and former director
at Harvard Business School Executive Education

" *This book is fantastic for practitioners; it is simple, concise, and focused on action. Barbara articulates the problem, explains the science, shows best practices, and provides solutions. She lays out the research in a way that is easy to follow in order to set the tone for evidence-based practice. Plus, she makes it easy to review the book for quick tips by including summary points and potential actions for each chapter. The key to making lasting, meaningful change in equity, diversity, and inclusion is to take a comprehensive, strategic approach to systemic change, and Barbara's book provides readers with the foundation to initiate their strategic plan."*

—Tie Wang-Jones, dual PhD in Clinical Psychology
and Industrial-Organizational Psychology;
Global Matrix Leader, Diversity & Inclusion at IKEA Group

" *A stellar resource for understanding workforce diversity in the 21st century and a practical guide on* how *to maximize the full creativity and innovation of people from all different backgrounds.*"

—Joseph P. Gaspero, CEO and Co-Founder
at Center for Healthcare Innovation

" *Progress on diversity and inclusiveness can only be made if we also take a systems approach to understanding organizational behavior. Dr. Adams has written a true practitioner's handbook that clearly lays out the science that underpins diversity and inclusion best practices, while also addressing the emotions that drive the 'will' to change.* Women, Minorities, & Other Extraordinary People *skillfully reframes the journey ahead through an organizational lens, highlighting the importance of cultural norms, challenging misconceptions, and providing research and practical tools. The business case for diversity is more critical than ever, but it's not our only tool; as Dr. Adams establishes, 'if logic makes people think, emotions make people act.' This is a book for every practitioner's and leader's bookshelf.*"

—Jennifer Brown, author of *Inclusion: Diversity, the New Workplace, and the Will to Change*

" *Dr. Adams challenges many long-held hiring myths; that diverse talent simply isn't available; that diversity and inclusion issues and gaps can't be remedied. This book helps confront bias, reframes thinking, and provides companies with the framework and tools to implement an inclusion strategy that benefits employees, leaders, and shareholders.*"

—PJ Moore, Senior Vice President at CGI,
former Executive of Chase and IBM

Women,
Minorities,
& Other
Extraordinary
People

The New Path for
WORKFORCE DIVERSITY

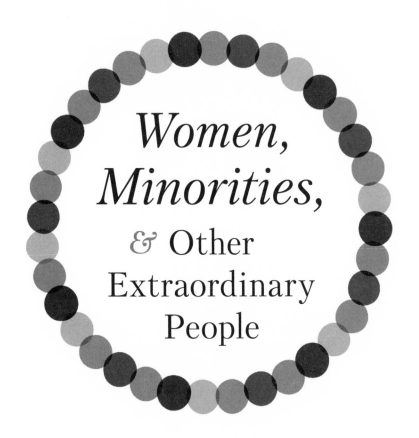

Women,
Minorities,
& Other
Extraordinary
People

BARBARA B. ADAMS, PsyD

GREENLEAF
BOOK GROUP PRESS

Published by Greenleaf Book Group Press
Austin, Texas
www.gbgpress.com

Distributed by Greenleaf Book Group

For ordering information or special discounts for bulk purchases, please contact Greenleaf Book Group at PO Box 91869, Austin, TX 78709, 512.891.6100.

Design and composition by Greenleaf Book Group
Cover design by Greenleaf Book Group

Grateful acknowledgment is made to the following sources for permission to reproduce copyrighted material:

From "The Miniature Guide to Critical Thinking, Concepts and Tools," by Dr. Richard Paul and Dr. Linda Elder, 7th Edition. Copyright © 2014 by the Foundation for Critical Thinking, www.criticalthinking.org. All rights reserved. Reproduced by permission of the Foundation for Critical Thinking.

For a continuation of credits, please see page "Permissions Credits (continued)" on page 240, which serves as an extension of the copyright page.

Publisher's Cataloging-in-Publication data is available.

Print ISBN: 978-1-62634-506-5

eBook ISBN: 978-1-62634-508-9

Part of the Tree Neutral® program, which offsets the number of trees consumed in the production and printing of this book by taking proactive steps, such as planting trees in direct proportion to the number of trees used: www.treeneutral.com

TreeNeutral

Printed in the United States of America on acid-free paper

18 19 20 21 22 23   10 9 8 7 6 5 4 3 2 1

First Edition

DEDICATION

For Paul, my smart, patient, thoughtful, creative husband
who never wavered in his belief about the importance of
this book and my ability to deliver on it. Your support and
encouragement are invaluable to me. I love you.

And

For my parents, who in the late 1960s, fulfilled my
holiday wish for the first black Barbie dolls. You told me
that other people might have unkind reactions to these
toys and reminded me that skin color may be different
among people, but we are all equal human beings.

Good job, Kath and Joe.

Contents

Introduction

*Our lives begin to end the day we become
silent about things that matter.*

—Rev. Dr. Martin Luther King, Jr.

Workforce diversity is good business. Studies show that companies with higher percentages of women in management roles have higher financial returns; ethnically diverse companies are more likely to outperform companies that struggle with diversity; companies with greater ethnic and gender diversity innovate faster; and improved gender diversity alone can add trillions of dollars to the global GDP.

More and more, organizations are beginning to think about change and the way that inclusive diversity offers not only a powerful economic advantage but also a better way to do business.

You can see it in the headlines:[1]

"Why hiring from all walks of life is the key to success" *(Inc.)*

"Everybody wins when employers embrace diversity" *(The Guardian)*

"Diversity leadership the accelerated quest for corporate winners" *(R News)*

"Diversity Dialogues Promote Discussion, Inclusivity" *(The Spectrum)*

"The business of diversity: how a diverse workforce makes money" *(Information Age)*

People are talking about workforce diversity and beginning to recognize its importance and relevance. At the same time, they're looking for guidance about how to *do* something about it in order to bring about needed change. When the way we've done business, set up structures and processes around what we do, and hired our workforces no longer represents the kinds of organizations we want to be, how do we step out of our old business models and mindsets? How do we begin to walk a new path of diversity and inclusion that enables us to achieve growth, heighten performance, and increase innovation?

Workforce Diversity Makes Sense

On an intuitive level, workforce diversity makes a lot of sense. When different types of people with different life experiences come together to collectively generate different kinds of ideas, they produce far more ideas than a like-minded group with similar experiences might. In most cases, more ideas are better because they can lead to faster and more creative innovations. And research shows these faster and more creative innovations are paving the way for companies to reach unprecedented growth on a global scale.

> ❝ *The business value of diversity and inclusion is widely documented, with significant data to support the idea that diverse, inclusive teams consistently outperform homogeneous teams to propel companies toward business success."*

On a statistical level, the business value of diversity and inclusion is widely documented, with significant data to support the idea that diverse, inclusive teams consistently outperform homogeneous teams to propel companies toward business success. The numbers show that diverse teams drive measurable increases in company performance. Catalyst, an organization that promotes inclusive workplaces for women, for example, reported that companies with three or more women on the board of directors had an increased performance of 53% return on equity, 42% return on sales, and 66% return on invested capital.[2]

McKinsey & Company, an established, well-respected consulting firm, released a report called *Diversity Matters,* which examined data for 366 companies spanning various industries in Canada, Latin America, the United Kingdom, and the United States. This study found that ethnically diverse companies are 35% more likely to outperform their respective national industry medians.[3]

The research is plentiful and vigorous.[4] Companies with greater ethnic and gender diversity innovate faster and perform better financially. Companies that pass stringent assessments of talent management, leadership accountability, and supplier diversity in the annual *DiversityInc* Top 50 survey all exist as proof of the great value of workforce diversity as a business strategy that drives success.[5]

Yet for all the well-documented benefits of workforce diversity, modern prejudice and groupthink are alive and well in many businesses today, even in Silicon Valley, the place that purports to value difference, to be different, and to think differently. Businesses that recognize the importance of and even champion workforce diversity and inclusion are usually unable to overcome the culture and mindset that make this work, let alone be sustainable. Companies that are interested in bringing about change inevitably find that they come up against obstacles they are ill equipped to handle.

Changing the Way We Work

Inclusive diversity offers a huge business advantage and can literally transform a company. But it's difficult to attain and, honestly, is about more than just economic benefit. This book is for anyone who wants change in the workplace and knows their companies could be and do more. It's for business leaders, hiring managers, those who work in human resources and people operations, and all those within an organization who believe things can be done differently. What you'll read in these pages is not for the faint of heart.

The ideas I introduce will require you to step forward to validate challenges people have faced, cause those around you to think in a new way, and motivate individuals in your spheres of influence to self-reflect and shift their patterns of behavior.

> 66 *This book is for anyone who wants change in the workplace and knows their companies could be and do more. It's for business leaders, hiring managers, those who work in human resources and people operations, and all those within an organization who believe things can be done differently.*"

I've been helping companies create systemic processes of change for over twenty years. I specialize in managed behavior change; and as an organization development expert in diversity, I've seen firsthand the economic and moral crisis in businesses and industries across the globe when our workforces fail at inclusion. Gender, race, and age are just three of many dimensions of difference; but our physical abilities, sexual orientation, socioeconomic status, ancestry, education, work experience, and more all comprise the diverse dimensions we have as human beings. My mission is to advance a new path for workforce diversity, equity,

and inclusion, by embracing all of the complex multidimensional layers we bring to the workplace.

This book will help you and your company create an inclusive work environment by maximizing the value that differences in people bring to the workforce. I'll offer key steps for developing a diverse and inclusive workforce and help you with the process of change.

I've worked in technology, healthcare, financial services, and with government clients both in the United States and internationally. I've seen companies thrive, prosper, and grow, and other ones stagnate and perform poorly. What I observed in the successful organizations inspired me to develop many of the ideas I present in this book.

> 66 *This book will help you and your company create an inclusive work environment by maximizing the value that differences in people bring to the workforce."*

I believe we have it within ourselves to act courageously, work differently, and really make a change for the betterment of ourselves, our workplaces, and our society. I believe there's hope for us in the way we do business and the way we live. But we have our work cut out for us.

The solutions in this book will call for us to be brave, resolute leaders in business environments where change can be hard to come by.

A Crisis in Our Companies

In 2014, the technology industry owned up to its lack of diversity, at last providing evidence and issuing apologies aplenty. Google

started the public confessional first, followed by Facebook, Twitter, LinkedIn, Apple, Yahoo, eBay, and myriad other companies. All of them communicated the same message:

- We know we are woefully behind in achieving our diversity goals.
- We have a lot of work to do to make diversity in the workforce real.
- We are implementing initiatives to address the issue.

The public also heard companies lament the difficulty of finding qualified candidates to hire, especially the challenges inherent in locating female and minority individuals with science and engineering degrees.

And yet three years later, by 2017, can you guess the measured increase in workforce diversity that came out of all the new initiatives those companies implemented? Sorry to say, it was nearly zero.

When asked why, companies responded that the lack of qualified women and minority candidates stems from deeply entrenched, historical issues that took years to create and that will take many more years to resolve. This winds up being a convenient and all-too-familiar excuse, even when companies have the best of intentions. The blame game goes something like this: girls are discouraged by parents and teachers from pursuing technical careers; too few African-Americans and Latinos take Advanced Placement courses in high school; unconscious biases lead us to hire those who look like we do. While there's some truth to all of this, it's also true that the attrition rates of female and minority recruits are unusually high in many tech companies, which have often done a poor job of hiring and retaining women and minorities, even for nontechnical roles.

During this time, not one tech company willingly came forward to publicly disclose its poor diversity numbers until prompted by civil rights advocates, who repeatedly and persistently showed up at shareholder meetings and publicly requested the release of this data. After Google came clean, other companies felt safer and began to disclose their information as well.

Technology companies are, of course, not alone in dealing with the ongoing problem of an overly homogeneous workforce. Women's lack of progress in securing top jobs and a widespread lack of opportunity for people of color have been perpetual challenges in many industries for decades. More than forty years have passed since significant numbers of women began arriving in the corporate workforce; over thirty years have passed since the now-famous "glass ceiling" was first identified by Gay Bryant, editor of *Working Woman* magazine. Passage of the initial equal pay laws in the United States occurred more than fifty years ago.[6] And Civil Rights legislation, designed to provide equal access and opportunities to African-Americans and other underrepresented minorities, was also enacted more than fifty years ago.

Discrimination Is Real

So how are things looking for women and minorities today? Honestly, they're not looking so good. In late 2015, LeanIn.org and McKinsey & Company partnered together to undertake and publish a comprehensive study, composed of data from over 100 companies and nearly 30,000 employees. They titled it *Women in the Workplace*, and the findings were extremely troubling, revealing that corporate America's path to gender equality is progressing at a pace so slow that it will take more than 100 years before women achieve parity with men in executive roles, and at least 25

years for women just to reach parity at the Senior Vice President level. This study validates that barriers to advancement are real, for both white women and women of color, who are underrepresented at every organizational level.[7]

Gender Barriers at Work

You probably know some of the standard explanations for the disparity in numbers between men versus women in power positions in companies. These include the ideas that:

- Childcare and eldercare responsibilities typically and primarily fall to women;
- Communication styles are just different for men and women; and
- We all possess implicit biases that lead us to unintentionally discriminate, causing us to more frequently hire and promote those who look and act like us.

The sociologist Kristen Schilt, in her book *Just One of the Guys? Transgender Men and the Persistence of Gender Inequality,* interviews dozens of transgender people. Their perspectives and experiences validate that the barriers for women in the workplace are substantial.

Schilt found that individuals who were already established in their careers before they transitioned from female to male experienced that as men, they were presumed competent. And they noted that before transitioning, as women, they were presumed either less competent or incompetent until they proved themselves otherwise. They also experienced that advice given by men in the workplace was taken more seriously than advice given by women.

Overall, Schilt's study attests to the fact that in the workplace, gender stereotypes are real and continue to favor masculine over feminine. She offers a unique perspective, that of the experience of both female and male perspectives emanating from the same person, validating the reality of gender discrimination in the workplace and revealing the problem of a deeply entrenched patriarchy that is a barrier to women.[8]

The Problem with Our Mindsets

Many organizations have attempted to make diversity a priority by setting robust targets for promoting women and persons of color to leadership roles. They have required that diverse candidate slates be considered for senior positions and have invested in mentoring and sponsorship efforts to develop internal talent. Yet, their pipelines still don't show the desired level of improvement in diversity.

Diversity is a noun meaning "the mix," whereas *inclusion* is a noun meaning "making the mix work." Inclusion refers to proactive behaviors we take based on self-awareness and respect for difference that make people feel valued for the abilities, unique qualities, and perspectives they contribute to an organization. Enhanced social inclusion holds a large part of the answer to the challenge of developing marvelously diverse, productive, engaging businesses. Enhanced social inclusion at work is the process of improving the terms on which individuals and groups participate and contribute value to the organization. It's about enhancing opportunities for interaction with women and minorities, people who typically are excluded from all that white men get to do.

" Diversity *is a noun meaning 'the mix,' whereas* inclusion *is a noun meaning 'making the mix work.'*"

In spite of what the Supreme Court has ruled, a company is *not* a person.[9] *People* make up companies, and they warrant the developmental opportunities to reflect on the sources of their beliefs, their assumptions about others, and their individual roles in supporting the structures (no matter how unintended or subconscious) that keep women and minorities held back in the organizations they work for. Only then will corporate efforts be able to succeed.

If individual employees do not possess belief systems that work inclusively, then a diverse, inclusive workplace can never truly develop. The charge is to transform the nature of employee and leadership development so that the company will change. Individual and collective thought processes need to expand for organizational systems and policies to change and for a company's diversity and inclusion results to improve in a meaningful and sustainable way. People must change for companies to change. It is not possible for this to work in any other order. We have fifty years of proof.

" *People must change for companies to change.*"

If diversity and inclusion are to evolve, there must be continuous improvement, learning, and adaptation of the concept. The attempt over the past decades to be "color-blind" and "treat everyone the same," however well-intentioned, has really only resulted in an increased amount of discrimination. The United States has long been referred to as a "melting pot," meaning that immigrants from many different parts of the world arrive on American shores

and can assimilate into mainstream American culture. But in this model, we wind up minimizing or rejecting differences among groups, and the pretense of sameness is projected. In reality, if we were to truly accept, appreciate, and value differences among people, American society might instead be described more as a "salad bowl," with different tastes, colors, and shapes that offer positive value, either separately or together. Which do you prefer? A bowl of tomatoes or an entire mixed salad? A row of hammers or an entire set of tools? A homogeneous team or a diverse team?

Having the choice of tomatoes or a mixed salad demonstrates the appeal of variety. The preference for multiple tools versus only hammers is easy. Why settle for just one function when you can choose from lots of other functions? By that same token, once you appreciate and value the performance power of a diverse team, why select anything else?

A New Narrative

A new narrative that binds diversity and inclusion to an organization's business strategy holds great promise for our collective future. Yet, a commonly overlooked reason for a lack of diversity, particularly in business, is the failure to develop and align diversity, equity, inclusion, and cultural awareness with the strategic priorities that support the company's mission. If the founders did not emphasize the value of a diverse and inclusive workforce in the original organizational DNA, then it would be especially difficult to develop a preference for diversity and inclusion later on.

No framework yet exists for effectively and meaningfully navigating differences among people. Yet developing and implementing this inclusive mindset is critical to succeeding in the diversity and

inclusion—D&I—space. When employees in a company feel that they're in a psychologically safe environment, they'll feel freer to express their viewpoints and ideas. And this diverse input can enable companies to consider a much broader array of business situations. Discovering innovative designs, better understanding potential new markets, and having a more engaged workforce are tremendous potential benefits to all of this.

The Path to Address the Crisis

In the coming chapters, I'll show you that while developing and sustaining a diverse and inclusive workforce is challenging, it is *possible*. Those organizations that achieve and maintain this style of environment will survive and outperform their competition.

We're at a fascinating juncture in global business—when a company can be great today yet out of business tomorrow. And this ability to rise and fall so rapidly underscores the importance of building a diverse workforce and an inclusive environment at the inception of a company. These critical actions directly influence the ability of an organization to deliver on its mission and succeed long term.

The goals of this book are to explore the challenges of developing diverse, inclusive organizations, to share a framework for how to navigate difference, and to propose a new path. I also invite immediate action to begin resolving what appear to be complex issues but that actually have straightforward, tangible solutions, provided that company leaders possess the fortitude to explore their beliefs and examine the standards upon which their corporate cultures have been built. These leaders must be willing to examine the assumptions that drive their behaviors, apply their own learning to their organizations, take risks, and act with courage and enthusiasm.

Business benefits alone are insufficient to drive the implementation of a diverse and inclusive workforce. Companies that focus on "initiatives" to solve the problem but don't understand the value systems upon which company behavior is predicated will most assuredly lose the battle to hire and keep diverse talent—and with it, lose their competitive edge. Diversity initiatives focus on symptoms rather than root causes, making those initiatives insufficient at driving real, sustainable change.

❝ *Diversity initiatives focus on symptoms rather than root causes, making those initiatives insufficient at driving real, sustainable change.*"

Nothing will change until leaders and employees within organizations begin to engage in conversations about bias, personal and cultural beliefs, social structure, assumptions garnered from the experiences of their own lives, their awareness of others, and their willingness to suspend judgment and develop curiosity about what they don't know and innately fear: people who are different from them. And these differences extend far beyond gender, age, race, physical ability, or anything else visible. Typically, invisible differences include beliefs, perspectives, sexual orientation, religion, family status, military veteran status, value systems, skills, education, life experiences, thought processes, talents, and heritage.

Diverse and inclusive work environments can only be created if change first comes from within each person. What is workforce development, after all, if not self-development? And employees are increasingly favoring personal development over other types of benefits.[10] The desire for growth in emotional intelligence and self-awareness reflects the purpose-driven mindset of today's emerging workforce. Eighty percent of business professionals

believe companies have a responsibility to make a positive impact on society, beyond just making a profit, and that an inclusive, diverse company measurably boosts employee productivity.[11]

A reflective, mindful workforce, guided by inclusive leaders, will enable the means required for organizational systems and policies to change. Only then can a company realize and sustain the benefits of diversity and inclusion. How wonderful to watch a new narrative emerge so that companies can use the business value and competitive advantage of a diverse, inclusive, equitable, and more highly engaged workforce to personal, professional, and societal advantage.

CHAPTER ONE

Acknowledging the Problem, Embracing the Opportunity

Don't miss out on something that could be amazing,
just because it could be difficult.

—Source Unknown

Companies increasingly understand the business benefits of workforce diversity: higher profits, engaged employees, increased creativity, and innovation in products and services. But the way most organizations approach the challenge of developing workplaces filled with different kinds of people has not worked well for decades.

Incremental improvements in diversity are insufficient in a global marketplace where shifting demographics require a deeper appreciation of those who are different from us. As competition increases, the companies that succeed will be the ones that approach the opportunity for change with bold actions that alter mindsets to produce results. The problem is so significant and the opportunity so vast that we need special assistance to address resistance to change as it arises. Call it organizational therapy.

Organizational therapy addresses the study of dysfunction in workplace environments. This can take place at various company levels and span different functional areas. In business settings, people tend to downplay individual and team issues for fear of being seen as weak, unmanageable, or problematic. They worry that it's dangerous or unsafe to discuss the issues they need to address. Organizational psychologists often refer to these undiscussed issues as "the elephant in the room." Everyone knows the elephant is there—its presence is huge—but no one is brave enough or feels competent enough to discuss it. This naturally leads to suboptimal individual and group performance until a process is created to manage these challenging and often sensitive dialogues.

Organizational therapy is a lot like individual therapy in three respects: you have to acknowledge the existence of an issue or problem; you have to want to change it; and you have to be willing to do the (potentially uncomfortable) work. Acknowledging we have a problem in our companies—and that the problem is real—requires us to admit that the lack of diversity in businesses today has not been fixed by laws, policies, regulations, or education and training programs. So much effort has been expended to try and make changes over the years, and that's why it's painful to need to own up to the fact that all this effort has not removed the problem.

Just over 1,800 companies compete annually for a spot on the *DiversityInc* Top 50 Companies for Diversity survey, now (at the time of this writing) in its 17th year. This is the premier competition for companies working hard to improve equity, diversity, and inclusion in their organizations—and seeking public recognition for doing so. But 1,800 entrants is a low number when you consider that this number comes out of the eligible *2.8 million*

businesses in the United States alone that generate a sales revenue between 1 million and 1 billion or more dollars a year.[1]

This strongly suggests that few organizations, across multiple industries, truly understand how to successfully create and manage a diverse, inclusive workforce to obtain the benefits that having different perspectives brings. This is due in part to attitudes of indifference when it comes to the topic of diversity. Also, we often don't understand how prevalent our unconscious biases are; nor do we recognize the way these biases can impact our interactions with others. Most organizations lack even a shared framework for how to work with differences among people.

Often, leaders of organizations logically know what the evidence states, but either don't know how to, or are not willing to, take action beyond so-called diversity initiatives for real improvement. These executives need the assistance, knowledge, and wisdom of a forward-thinking diversity and inclusion leader. Yet, too often diversity is relegated to being just another function of the Human Resources (HR) department. Company heads operate on false beliefs that initiatives alone will solve the problem. But in so doing, they wind up ignoring the systemic change and leadership required for long-term success. Initiatives can definitely address symptoms and may even provide short-term relief to issues such as lack of diversity. But in the end, initiatives will always be insufficient because they don't address the root causes—such as hidden bias and belief systems that are driven by illogical or irrational thought.

The Problem of Underrepresentation

Though issues of diversity and inclusion are prominent in the news, there remains a disparity in numbers that highlights the

ongoing crisis in our workforces. The Human Capital Report, produced by Mercer and the World Economic Forum, shows that of the eligible global female population, approximately 65% participate in the workforce, as compared to the larger 80% of males who participate in the workforce. Women currently represent less than 5% of Fortune 500 Chief Executive Officers, less than 25% of senior management, and only 19% of corporate board seats globally. And the data for Blacks, Latinos, and other underrepresented minority groups is as low as these numbers or even lower. We're unable to benefit from the differences, innovations, and advancements that women and minorities could bring to our companies; as a result, we are thwarting our own efforts to meaningfully grow our businesses.

66 *We're unable to benefit from the differences, innovations, and advancements that women and minorities could bring to our companies; as a result, we are thwarting our own efforts to meaningfully grow our businesses."*

Survey data from business school graduates in Asia, Canada, Europe, and the United States also shows that career aspirations, though equal among men, women, and minorities in their early years of employment, change drastically as people progress in their careers. Today, fifty years since the passage of the very Civil Rights legislation that was designed to provide equity to women and minorities, positions of leadership continue to be held primarily by white men. And the representation of women and minority candidates in leadership positions falls off precipitously at the midpoint of their career ladders, when childcare and eldercare responsibilities rise and career inertia sets in; this often leads them to exit the workforce entirely.

Creating receptive environments where women and minorities want to stay in their roles is an enormous challenge inside and outside the high-tech arena. This problem applies to every organization employing people who work in technical roles. The Center for Talent Innovation's report "Accelerating Female Talent in Science, Engineering & Technology (STEM)" reveals the challenge of retention. The report found that women in STEM positions are 45% more likely to quit within a year than men in similar jobs.[2]

In spite of increased access to higher education and equal pay, the positive influence of civil rights and diversity efforts, and the many studies that show a high return on investment (ROI) and increased profitability among companies with women and minorities in senior leadership roles, white males consistently attain and remain in positions of power.

But why? What hidden forces are driving these results?

The Problem with Unconscious Bias

Biologically, we're hardwired to prefer the company of those people who look and sound like us, and who share our interests, experiences, and values. Human evolution required the safety of tribes. Unconscious processes are instinctual to help humans survive. For example, in a public place, we often make snap judgments about who is safe to be with and who isn't. This instinct is designed to keep us from harm.

Yet, while these biases can be helpful, they can also cause us to make faulty assumptions. Social psychologists call this phenomenon *social categorization,* whereby we use intuition to automatically sort people into groups. And while we often use these categorizations effectively for objects, the categories we use to sort people are not actually logical or rational.

Research shows that 90% of brain function is automatic and outside conscious awareness. The human reflexive system controls our automatic processes—things that are immediate, require little effort, and occur spontaneously. These include our long-term memory, emotions, habits, bodily functions (like when we feel hungry or sleepy), and the need to innately categorize people and things as either safe or unsafe. The 10% of brain function that is not automatic, but which requires deliberate, conscious control, is called the reflective system. This part of the brain involves focus and time, and it requires our motivation to sustain deliberate effort. Our conscious mind governs short-term memory and enables us to analyze, think, and plan. Understanding these differences is vital, since the categories we use to sort people bypass our conscious mind, and live within our reflexive system or unconscious mind—the one responsible for keeping us safe—and lead to hidden biases.

Traditional thinking suggests that human bias and discrimination is intentional. This has been shown to be true in a small percentage of cases. But since 90% of brain functioning is automatic and outside conscious awareness, we know people will make biased decisions without even realizing it.

To make matters even more complicated, consider how our unconscious, discriminatory preferences stem from a combination of socialization, individual and group experience, and instinct that's unique to each of us. Thanks to science, today we understand that bias is normative, unconscious, and mostly unintentional.

Hidden Preferences

Over the past decade, I've attended many diversity conferences and listened to, participated in, and explored the topic of unconscious

bias, also referred to as *implicit* or *hidden* bias. At Harvard University in 2013, I heard Professor Mahzarin Banaji, an acclaimed social psychologist and one of the original developers of the Implicit Association Test, or IAT (the primary instrument used to measure unconscious bias), educate a diverse group of executives about the role that implicit biases play in our lives, and how these hidden preferences affect our behavior toward others. The IAT uncovers the biases we hold, but which do not reflect what we say we believe in. For example, most people view themselves as nice people, and not as prejudiced. Yet, the Race IAT shows us that 75% of people have an implicit preference for white people over Black people.[3]

A profound though distressing learning from this data is that being nice and being prejudiced are not discordant, nor contradictory. You can be a nice person and be prejudiced. In fact, three out of four people are. This is why "being a nice person" or "being a good person" are simply not enough to overcome racism, sexism, and other hidden biases.

66 *You can be a nice person and be prejudiced."*

We all have our own predilections. We all have unconscious or implicit bias. Frequently, however, our implicit biases do not reflect what we say we believe. As an example, I've long been enamored of older people. To me, they're living historians with entertaining and insightful stories to tell, and I typically really enjoy their company. But at one point when tested using the IAT, I was surprised to find that I harbor a negative association with the elderly.

In fact, of the millions of people who have their hidden biases uncovered, the data shows that 80% prefer young people to old

(presumably because "old" may carry a negative connotation). Similarly, most people do not consider themselves to be racially prejudiced and would strongly deny any suggestion of such. Yet, the data reveals that 75% of whites and Asians demonstrate a hidden preference for whites over Blacks. Equally perplexing is the knowledge that race does not affect results when testing for hidden bias. About 50% of Blacks who take the assessment have a greater preference for whites over Blacks.[4]

Culture and society hold strong influences on biases and beliefs. When certain groups are more associated with good things and other groups with bad things, people unwittingly believe these associations. So, for example, seeing whites portrayed as lawyers and Blacks portrayed as criminals on television and in the media subtly influences how individuals perceive these groups. The more positive associations one group has over another, the more profound the effect on society. These associations may not reflect what people say they believe or even think they believe. It's not that people are lying; it's simply that we all unconsciously make connections; and these hidden effects are impossible to escape in society—that is, until you train yourself to see them.

The Problem with Positive Bias

As odd as this may sound, positive biases can have just as profound a negative effect as negative biases. This idea can be quite hard to accept. It's as confounding as the knowledge that we all have, and often act on, negative biases about people who are not like us. And when we help others with whom we have relationships, we provide advantages to our "in-group," others who are like us.

If, for example, I provide a work reference for the child of my friend, who is white like me, I would unintentionally limit diversity by promoting the status quo, even though I'm simply intending to be helpful.

So how does a disadvantaged person, without these connections, access equal opportunities?

A Simple Act for Powerful Change

The universities I graduated from periodically solicit me for donations. When I am in a financial position to give, I happily do so. But last year I changed my practice and also gave an equal amount, at the same time, to the United Negro College Fund. It's a small but meaningful way for me to try to mitigate ongoing exclusionary "out-groups," which are groups one is not a member of or invited to join. Imagine if alumni donors from every institution of higher education also donated to organizations serving underrepresented communities. Powerful change could occur.

My thinking about discrimination as something that solely inflicts harm on others has changed, now that I understand that discrimination often, more subtly, results from the actions of helping people who are like me, which then serves to maintain an "out-group" and effectively limits diversity. The hiring processes in most companies contain three positive biases:

1. The first is educational attainment—where an applicant went to school and how well he or she did there. This

bias is perhaps the most egregious and limiting. Intel, an American multinational corporation ranked among the most valuable, most admired, most ethical, and top global brands, is led by CEO Brian Krzanich, a graduate of San Jose State University (SJSU). Although SJSU is a good school, it isn't considered a top-tier school. I once heard Mr. Krzanich share that for years he tried to hide that fact out of concern that his schooling would somehow be held against him. He doesn't hide it any longer because as a talented, successful person and a diversity champion, he understands that it's important for people to know that great talent doesn't come just from top-tier schools. Similarly, Tim Cook, the CEO of Apple, currently the most valuable company in the world, is a graduate of Auburn University (AU) in Alabama, once again considered to be a good but not top-tier school. Remember that great talent exists in many places, and not just in universities that have prestigious reputations.

2. The second is experience level, defined by how long a person has been in the workforce versus how long he or she has been in the job market.

3. The third and last are relationships encompassing how much of a network the applicant has established or how many people he or she can tap into for support, references, and other kinds of help.

These biases are driving hiring practices and netting the overly homogeneous workplaces that exist today. If diverse workforces are ever to develop, we need to examine and fundamentally

rethink our positive biases. This, of course, doesn't mean that it's wrong for us to be helpful when we're asked, only that it's critical not to favor only those with whom we have a connection, or who attended our alma mater, or who worked with us at a previous company, or with whom we feel comfortable. Positive biases are as destructive as negative biases, if not more so.

I've led workshops in which we openly explore the topic of unconscious bias. Inevitably, following these workshops, people ask, "If we all have these biases, at an unconscious level, what can be done about that? Aren't we at the mercy of our hidden beliefs?" It's a natural question but is problematic at its core. This victim mentality, in which people shrug, act indifferently, and passively acquiesce, only solidifies prejudicial behaviors.

66 *Positive biases are as destructive as negative biases, if not more so."*

But, if we heighten awareness of our individual biases, we can better enable a diversity of bias to develop. (This may be the best we can hope for.) For example, the Gender IAT shows that 76% of people more readily associate "male" with "career," and "female" with "family."[5] This means that 24% of people do not make this implicit association. Surfacing biases to ensure that leaders and teams at all organizational levels include people from the 76% category and the 24% category enables the development of teams where diversity of bias is present. This serves the purpose of countering the very preferences that lead us to gather in homogeneous teams, and supports a much greater possibility of innovation in the business environment. The following illustrates this concept:

Testing for Diversity of Bias

Fact: Data from Gender Implicit Association Tests shows that 76% of people more readily associate "males" with "career" and "females" with "family."

Company Goal: To advance more women into senior leadership roles over the next twenty-four months.

Action: A thirteen-member executive leadership team individually takes the Gender IAT.

Positive Result: Ten members of the executive leadership team are found to have an unconscious bias that associates "males" with "career" and "females" with "family," but three members are *not* found to have that bias. This is good; a diversity of bias exists. Move forward with the plans.

Negative Result: All thirteen members are found to have an unconscious bias that associates "males" with "career" and "females" with "family." This is not good. How will a team with 100% shared gender bias help advance women into senior leadership roles?

Project Implicit was created after the development of the IAT and is a nonprofit organization and global collaborative of researchers interested in the human thoughts and feelings that exist outside conscious awareness and control. The researchers call these types of thoughts and feelings *implicit social cognition.* We've learned, more than a decade of research into Project Implicit's findings, that:

- hidden biases are pervasive;
- people are mostly unaware of their biases;

- unconscious preferences predict human behavior; and
- individuals differ in their levels of hidden bias.

The good news is that since we know people differ in their levels of bias, we also know prejudice is malleable. As social structures and cultural environments shift, the opportunity for people to change attitudes toward others is made possible through experience and greater awareness of hidden influence as well as greater exposure to others with whom we differ.

    " *The good news is that since we know people differ in their levels of bias, we also know prejudice is malleable.*"

Making Contact

A body of research known as *Intergroup Conflict Theory*, first introduced by the psychologist Gordon Allport in the 1950s, aims to reduce or eliminate prejudice among different groups of people by providing enough contact between groups that everyone can become comfortable and even appreciative of each other. Allport's central premise includes the need for specific conditions to be present for this to work. People have to agree to engage equally in their developing relationship, share common goals, decide to have a facilitator or leader to support the interaction between the groups, and be willing to know one another on a personal level (friendship basis).[6] Consider how you might create similar conditions when you think about how to make contact and establish connections with different groups in your company.

Research psychologists from around the world also spent decades coming up with useful criteria needed for contact among groups to work. Fast-forward past the year 2000, and Thomas

Pettigrew, PhD, professor emeritus at the University of California at Santa Cruz, made a startling discovery. In a meta-analysis of 500 studies, he found that in all but the most hostile and dangerous conditions (in which people feel physically threatened with harm), the requirements for success don't matter—contact alone is enough to effect warm, positive feelings between different groups of people. The reason contact between different groups works, the studies imply, lies not in the head but in the heart. Pettigrew found that stereotypes about other people don't necessarily change with contact, but attitudes do. In other words, people grow to like one another just by being around one another.[7]

Gaining Exposure to Different Groups

I attend an event called the Black Enterprise TechConneXt Summit every year. My purpose in doing so is threefold: 1) the speakers are inspiring and help me recommit to my work, broadening and deepening my perspectives; 2) the event draws hundreds of talented Black people, which reaffirms my knowledge that there is no shortage of minority talent in technology (contrary to popular opinion); and 3) most importantly, I am one of perhaps ten to twelve white people in attendance, which provides me with the opportunity to feel what it's like to be a minority and to gain exposure to others of a different race. There are always a few people who look at me as if to say, "What is she doing here?" But most attendees are warm, welcoming, and curious about my presence at what they could justifiably call their event. It's a valuable experience for me, and one I recommend to others who genuinely want to grow in their understanding and appreciation of others who are different from them.

Organizations that want to improve workforce diversity and inclusion can take advantage of Pettigrew's discovery in a couple of ways. Many mid- to large-size companies have Employee Resource Groups (ERGs). ERGs are also referred to as Affinity Groups, Staff Associations, or other similar monikers. These groups form because of shared characteristics among members, and exist to provide support for business objectives and camaraderie among members. For example, it's common to have an African-American ERG, an Asian ERG, and a Latino ERG. Opportunities for social gatherings among groups provide chances for people of different races and ethnicities to know one another better. Similarly, there are thousands of professional organizations that people join based on interest. Here are just a few:

- Black Career Women's Network (bcwnetwork.com)
- National Association of Black Accountants (nabainc.org)
- National Urban League Young Professionals (nulyp.iamempowered.com)
- National Association of Asian American Professionals (naaap.org)
- Center for Asian Pacific American Women (apawomen.org)
- Association of Latino Professionals in Finance & Accounting (alpfa.org)
- Society for Advancement of Chicanos/Hispanics & Native Americans in Science (sacnas.org)
- Business & Professional Women Europe (bpw-europe.org)
- Canadian Association for Women in Business Network (womeninbiznetwork.com)
- The International Alliance for Women (tiaw.org)

While some of these associations have membership requirements, some do not, and most welcome guests. The opportunities abound for getting to know others not like ourselves. It takes only motivation and action to derive the significant benefits of those opportunities.

Creating Opportunities for Diversity and Inclusion

The diversity problem in companies cannot be solved by making token hires, giving money to school programs, or simply sending employees to unconscious-bias training. This is not about poor Equal Employment Opportunity (EEO) data that just simply counts the number of employees in different categories of race, gender, and disability. Excellent EEO numbers may in fact demonstrate compliant levels of diversity but not guarantee inclusive environments. There's a profound difference between diversity and inclusion, and trying to reach for one goal without the other shows only superficial commitment to change.

> " *There's a profound difference between diversity and inclusion, and trying to reach for one goal without the other shows only superficial commitment to change.*"

At its essence, diversity is about difference. We inherit our culture, religion, ethnicity, and family beliefs and learn them through the environments we were raised in, like schools or community centers. Workplace inclusion involves valuing individual differences in group settings. When employees with different experiences of the world, varying belief systems, and dissimilar upbringing in multicultural environments come together, they generate a multitude of

ideas. These ideas may be for problem solving, new product development, or enhanced service offerings. And it's this wealth of ideas that becomes the wellspring of innovation in business. Diversity alone can't accomplish this. Companies need to act inclusively and show respect for and curiosity about differences. It's easy to be inclusive without being diverse, for example, with a homogeneous group. But, working with similar people doesn't provide the fresh, new, more challenging perspectives that drive business success.

What Diverse and Inclusive Teams Can Prevent

Consider the Apple Watch. Advertised as the ultimate device for a healthy life, this product was designed to work best on light-skinned people. Buried deep in Apple's online disclosure forms is a list of so-called restricted chemicals for wearables. Sure enough, colorants are on the list, including but not limited to black and brown pigments. Following the hoopla around the initial product launch, hashtags like #BlackWristsMatter and #TattooGate exploded online.

And why not? One of the largest technology companies in the world, publicly called out for its lack of workforce diversity, launched a product that people realized would not function on individuals with dark skin or tattoos.[8] This embarrassment could have been avoided altogether had a diverse, inclusive team been responsible for the development and testing of the watch before its launch. But this was not the case. Perhaps the fair-skinned executives and workforce at Apple were surprised by their product's deficiency and the subsequent outcry by the public. But this is what can happen when people in companies see the world through the same lens.

Workplace diversity and inclusion are like the interconnected and interdependent forces of yin and yang that cannot be separated. Each is imperative to keep the people—and the company—functioning well.

Setting Your Company Up for Success

Talent management is the use of strategic planning, typically within human resources or people operations departments, to ensure the ability of companies to achieve their business goals. Having a diverse, inclusive workforce directly affects the ability of a company to perform well. Talent management and a diverse and inclusive workforce are effectively two sides of the same coin. Therefore, leaders need to ask if the present success of their organizations is sustainable over time without a change in the policies and practices that maintain sameness.

Will the current, homogeneous status quo of most organizations ensure the kind of innovation that will drive future success? It's unlikely. There can be a great deal of comfort when people feel an easy "fit" with others; like-mindedness creates feelings of support and belonging that hold great appeal. Psychologists call this *affinity bias*. While there's nothing necessarily wrong with affinity bias in and of itself, it can be a huge liability in business. When this happens, human beings do not naturally gravitate toward those who are different; rather, they seek comfort and perceive safety in those whom they deem to be like themselves. And unfortunately, in most large companies today, affinity bias is deeply entrenched in the systems and policies already in place, which hinders the ability of an organization to become inclusive. To change, companies first need to provide environments in which people feel a sense of psychological safety.

Providing a Safe Place

We've discussed many of the virtues and benefits of diverse and inclusive workforces, and it's important to communicate these to others. At the same time, people need you to not only help guide them in their thinking and learning about this but also create a dynamic that enables them to feel safe and positive about doing the hard and necessary work of making change happen. With so many obstacles already in the way, how do you encourage, challenge, motivate, and embolden people? How do you foster an environment that connects people with doing the good, right thing? And how do you create a space of psychological safety, where workers feel simultaneously challenged in their jobs while also feeling safe when exploring risk-taking ideas or minority viewpoints?

One simple way to help people feel comfortable with being themselves at work is to cease expecting them to subordinate themselves to the corporate identity. The people who work at Google are Googlers. The employees at Microsoft are called Microsofties. At Twitter, you're a Tweep. If you work at Amazon, you're an Amazonian. However, at Apple and many other companies, there are no set names employees go by, which helps emphasize the individuality and uniqueness of each person.

Creating a Speaking-Up Culture

A psychologically safe culture is one that is also termed a *speaking-up culture*. During the time I spent working in a large San Francisco-based hospital, we implemented something called Highly Reliable Surgical Teams (HRSTs). These teams underwent extensive specialized training so that any

Continued

member of the team—from the senior-ranking surgeon to the lower-level technician—could safely speak to one another. If they detected something amiss—for example, if there was a question about the count of sponges retrieved during an operation—anyone could ask the surgeon to double-check, and the doctor would do so and say "thank you." This was built into the culture of the hospital.

This is what hearing a minority viewpoint sounds like. It comes from an inclusive team, unafraid to ask questions, functioning in an environment without fear of repercussion.

Beginning to Engage

Apathy toward diversity in organizations is a common barrier to change. You can begin to break this barrier down by asking questions that, however uncomfortable to discuss at first, will serve to create engagement with the topic and allow people to acknowledge their indifference. Discussion groups could cover topics and questions such as:

- People can't be viewed through one lens. There's personality, age, race, gender, sexual orientation, physical ability, mental ability, and ethnicity. But there's also marital status, parental status, educational background, religion, recreational habits, and income level. Add in management status (or lack thereof) at work, the type of work one does, the functional group or department one is part of, and the geography one lives and works in. How do people primarily think of themselves? As a parent? An engineer? A leader? Why? And do we consider our values "the norm"? How accepting are we of those whose values differ from our own?

- What diversity means to us and how that is different from or the same as how our company defines diversity.

- Why the organization seems to have a really big focus on becoming more diverse. How can employees support it? Who do people talk to if they feel uncomfortable about it?

- Why it's important for us to care about inclusion, even if we're nice to everyone.

Engaging employees in early dialogue sets a context for how an organization defines diversity and inclusion and why it matters to the business and its leaders. It also sends the message that the company wants diversity and inclusion to matter to its employees, too. Helping people explore self-awareness builds the platform through which they can explore cultural awareness. This sets them up to better be able to communicate as the workforce becomes increasingly diverse. Early engagement helps mitigate resistance to diversity. Ultimately, it not only readies people to expand their cultural humility, which is an underlying requirement for learning, but also helps them grow in their willingness to adapt to change and remain relevant. They become better managers and better people.

Redesigning Your Work Environment

Interestingly, there are behavioral incentives you can introduce and implement in organizations with homogeneous workforces. Lessons from structural public health, for example, teach us that if an elevator in a building is hard to find but the stairway is prominently located, people will in fact take the stairs even though that means greater physical exertion. Similarly, we've learned that neighborhoods

with more sidewalks or bike paths encourage a greater number of people to use them. These are called "availability and accessibility interventions,"[9] and they show that you can actually prime desirable behaviors through environmental design. This means you can also influence the systems and policies that drive behaviors.

66 *You can also influence the systems and policies that drive behaviors. "*

Research shows that even changes as simple as music selection can influence behaviors. In one study, when German music was played in a supermarket, shoppers purchased more German wine. When French music was played, shoppers purchased more French wine.[10] Many so-called progressive companies boast about their nonhierarchical, flexible, and comfortable environments, yet in actuality they have overly homogeneous employee populations.

Imagine if you could do something so simple as to redesign the work environment to support difference instead of sameness, to promote diversity in a positive way. You could adorn the walls with photos of female and minority scientists and their accomplishments. You could offer screen savers with images that challenge common stereotypical associations, featuring men at home with children, women working at construction sites, people in wheelchairs coding at computers. Think of what adds to the culture and environment you're trying to create—wall colors, music selection, anything that inspires positive, desired behaviors, which embrace diversity and inclusion. It's fascinating to think that even just redesigning physical work environments can promote positive changes in the workforce if you do it thoughtfully and meaningfully.

How paradoxical it is that human beings feel comfortable with people who are like them yet must be with people who are

not like them in order to be able to develop, innovate, and thrive. To succeed in creating genuinely diverse and inclusive workforces, company leaders really need to learn how to navigate the unfamiliar territory that comes with valuing differences in people. And a skilled senior-level Chief Diversity and Inclusion Officer, in collaboration with a diverse board of directors and an inclusive CEO, knows how to do this and much more. Whether they're beginning the process of engaging people in conversation, asking employees to try stepping out of comfort zones, finding ways to create safe spaces, or even trying new ways of redesigning physical environments, these individuals can help organizations move toward diversity and inclusivity, beginning to change the systems, structures, and beliefs that have been holding people back.

" *How paradoxical it is that human beings feel comfortable with people who are like them yet must be with people who are not like them in order to be able to develop, innovate, and thrive.*"

Taking the First Step in Reaching Out

In late 2014, I delivered a keynote address at a conference in Northern California. By luck or planning, my talk happened to be preceded by Amy Roloff, star of the reality television series *Little People, Big World*. During her talk, Amy, who has achondroplasia dwarfism, talked about her family's decision to participate in the TV series as an opportunity to help teach viewers that being little is different, not deficient. She told moving stories about the challenges she faces every time

Continued

she walks into a room filled with "normal"-sized people, who often ignore her, and in so doing, create a situation that requires her to make the initial effort to start a conversation. Even then, she told us she's often met with negative reactions from visibly uncomfortable people who seem to look around, seeking ways to disengage with her.

Since my talk followed Amy's, I took the opportunity to explore the discomfort that "normal"-sized people feel and the assumptions we make about others who are different from us. I also talked about the advantage we have when we look like most other people and the responsibility we have to welcome those whose appearances are different. Amy's talk highlighted the fact that the onus for involvement should not lie solely on the person who is different from the group. Instead, it's important for us to remember that those with a clear but unearned advantage should be the first to extend a welcome.

Creating a New Kind of Organizational Chart

The learning and continuous improvement that's essential to advance diversity and inclusion (D&I) in companies requires commitment from a diverse board of directors, inclusive leadership from the chief executive officer, and the appointment or hiring of a chief diversity and inclusion officer (CDIO) in order to champion and exemplify the organizational dedication to this work. A dynamic CDIO can measure the inclusiveness of the CEO as a leader and help him or her develop accordingly. The CDIO can calculate the cost of the status quo, and develop and communicate a company's business case for diversity and inclusion. This person can educate the board of directors and the entire

organization on managing hidden bias, developing cultural curiosity, and understanding the power of self-reflection and beliefs. This individual can even lead a redesign of the physical work environment in order to support differences among people.

A Diverse Board

I recall feeling happily stunned when I first saw a one-page depiction of the board of directors of Kaiser Foundation Hospitals and Health Plan. The display had no words, no names, no titles, just professional photographs of each member. It was brilliant! The header on the slide was something like "A Diverse Board," and looking at the individual photos together on a single page exemplified the diversity of the group. Anyone looking at the group picture immediately saw the presence of women, Blacks, Asians, and younger and older people—a visual depiction of a diverse board of directors.

Khan Academy, an organization dedicated to providing free world-class education to anyone, has organized the online display of its governance boards in a similar way. Suppose every organization that states its commitment to diversity were to publish a similar view of their Annual Report on their company website. A simple, powerful new kind of organizational chart would be born, one that would illustrate what real commitment to diversity at the most senior level looks like.

Businesses are beginning an important conversation with the goal of understanding that different does not equal deficient if you purposefully remove judgment from the equation and work to mainstream cultural curiosity throughout your

Continued

company. The possibility of a new narrative for our collective future will develop organizations that are more inclusive of diverse talent, and hence better equipped to survive and prosper in a constantly changing world marketplace.

Recognizing That There's Emotion Involved

Business decisions are not made on logic alone. Political scientist and economist Scott Page wrote a powerful book called *The Difference: How the Power of Diversity Creates Better Groups, Firms, Schools, and Societies.* In it he shares compelling models that attest to the power of diversity. A diverse and inclusive workforce, he says, adds to the strength of an enlightened organization's bottom line, meaning it's good for business.[11] Throughout his book he presents evidence that's hard to refute. But why is building, having, and sustaining a diverse and inclusive workforce such a seemingly difficult thing? Why don't we see more companies doing this? Doesn't it just make sense?

I recently searched for scholarly literature by going to a database and entering the keywords "diversity," "performance," and "teams." The search results cited hundreds of papers, with the majority of them providing evidence to support the idea that diverse and inclusive teams consistently outperform homogeneous teams. You'd think that logically, with all things considered, just the amount of qualitative and quantitative data combined would be enough to compel company leaders to do everything possible to build diverse and inclusive workforces.

This would, as we know, help ensure business viability, positive outcomes, profitability, and growth for their companies. But if important decisions like these were made based only on logic and evidence, wouldn't it seem a less daunting endeavor to build a

diverse, inclusive workforce? Wouldn't the need to take action be obvious on a practical, rational, and even analytical level? Honestly, it would probably be considered ridiculous *not* to move forward with change. And yet, fifty years later, that's exactly where we still are today.

> " *Business decisions are not made based on logic alone. Emotions, assumptions, and hidden beliefs also drive behavior.* "

Clearly, business decisions are not made based on logic alone. Emotions, assumptions, and hidden beliefs also drive behavior. More often than not, however, we encounter people who tend to think of themselves as individuals who engage and leverage mostly logical, rational thought in their daily decision-making. Businesspeople, particularly those running mid- to large-size companies, seem to operate on the belief that emotions don't belong in credible workplace decision-making; they presume that emotions are likely to skew rational thought processes. Women especially have been historically and often stereotypically seen as more highly emotive than men, and as needing to learn to leave feelings out of business decisions. In large part, emotions have long been considered as separate and distinct from rational thought and therefore as best left out of critical business decisions. You'll see, again and again, ways in which logic is widely thought of as positive, and emotion as negative, in most decision-making.

But is this simplistic positive-negative mapping actually supported by evidence, or is it a widespread assumption that deserves a detailed examination? Are human emotions simply brain circuitry that distort sound, valid reasoning? Or is this a worldview from a time long ago?

Thoughts and Feelings Are Interconnected

The 1500s were a time in history known as the Enlightenment, which represented the birth of modernity. It blew religion out of the water, as progressive thinkers like John Locke
advanced the idea that individuals can think for themselves.
People became focused on the rational, and the quest for
finding "objective truth" via the scientific method became
the commonly accepted worldview.

By the 1800s, thinkers like Max Weber and Karl Marx
began looking at power structures in both societies and
businesses and the value of metrics and analysis. During the
Enlightenment, the underlying assumptions about the scientific method included the idea that there is an "objective
truth," that the rational is superior to the emotional, that lived
experience is not equal to objective truth, and that measurement is everything. But this is not fact; these assumptions
and beliefs represent a *worldview*, not an absolute truth.

Newly discovered biological evidence is beginning
to dismantle many beliefs about the affirmative power of
"pure" rational thought. In fact, research studies in neuroscience show us that emotion (and hidden beliefs that drive
emotion) can't really be separated from logic, and that
together the two comprise the primary functions in most
decision-making. Humans are both implicitly and explic-
itly influenced by beliefs they've developed and gathered
throughout life. Experiences that evoke our emotions–those
we remember as well as those we've long forgotten yet
stored in our brains–*combined* with rational thought are
used in an intricately connected way that defies separation
in human decision-making. I mention this so you can see the

important role that both logical, rational thinking and emotion play in the way people do business.

Two professors and authors, Hans-Rudiger Pfister and Gisela Bohm at the University of Bergen in Norway, have studied this quite a bit. They've specifically found that emotions don't imply irrationality, *and* that emotions are actually ubiquitous in decision-making. For us, this implies something about the integral role emotions play in business. The authors developed a four-part classification of how emotions function when people make decisions, demystifying for us what may actually be happening when people simply come across as "emotional" in our workplaces. The framework these scientists have created recognizes that emotions are inherently *melded* in rational thought, rather than just limited to being an *influence* on rational thought when decisions are made.

In business, we've traditionally believed that if leaders, managers, and workers behave rationally, then optimal decisions will be made, and that allowing emotions into the process will negatively influence these optimal choices. Yet this has been proven to be false. Neuroscience is increasingly demonstrating that emotion has been intricately melded with logic all along.

Why is it so important that we stop considering emotion as a threat to rationality? First, because emotion matters in business. People are happiest and most productive at work when they *feel* commitment to and passion for the services or products they're producing and the teams they're collaborating with. Customers who love certain products, and often the companies that produce them, *feel* trust and a sense of having received great value from their purchases.

❝ *Emotion matters in business. People are happiest and most productive at work when they feel commitment to and passion for the services or products they're producing and the teams they're collaborating with.*❞

Amazon is a huge company that didn't make a profit for over a decade. But today, many of its employees feel that they work for a cutting-edge organization, and customers feel satisfied that they can locate virtually any product on its site, use their Amazon Prime, and pay little to nothing to have what they need shipped. Many people love the products and services Amazon provides. Data-driven, relevant, measurable criteria usually suggest that any type of business that bleeds losses for over a decade should really be out of business. Amazon's Las Vegas–style bet, coupled with its early entry into cloud-based services, is paying off superbly now.

Feelings matter in business and in life. A growing body of evidence shows that optimal decision-making *requires* emotion, and that neurologically, a distinction between logical, cognitive processing and emotion may not actually even exist.[12] This is important, because feelings, both hidden and surfaced, keep leaders from developing the diverse, inclusive workforces they claim to logically understand the need for—and desire.

❝ *Feelings matter in business and in life.*❞

Logic makes people think. Emotion makes people act. Our will is attached to our emotions, not our intellect. Most leaders may consciously believe in equal opportunity and stand opposed to racism, sexism, homophobia, and other forms of discrimination. Yet, unconsciously they have biases that undermine their

stated beliefs about fairness and equality. Good intentions, from anyone and everyone in the workforce, guarantee zero immunity from hidden bias and unconscious prejudice.

" *Logic makes people think. Emotion makes people act.* "

Leveraging Our Differences

Let's talk about women and men and how they're different by design. Evolutionary biology makes this so. In the human brain, the anterior cingulate cortex (ACC), which considers options and makes decisions, is larger in women than in men. The prefrontal cortex (PFC), which helps control emotions and modulate the amygdala, is larger in women and matures faster in teen girls than in boys. The insula, also larger with heightened activity in women, processes intuition or gut feelings, and the hypothalamus, which oversees and regulates hormones, develops earlier in females.

Now, something for the guys: the amygdala is larger in men and widely known for producing the fight-or-flight response. The amygdala requires the PFC to keep it in check. The pituitary gland guides nurturing behavior for mommies and daddies, and the hippocampus, which is larger and more active in women than men, remembers emotional encounters, encompassing everything from arguments to romantic moments.

Simply stated, along with a host of other hormones, women are fueled by estrogen, and men are fueled by testosterone.[13]

Continued

For decades, people have actively worked to minimize or ignore the extent of male-female differences, while periodically celebrating clarifying works, such as Deborah Tannen's *You Just Don't Understand: Women and Men in Conversation* or John Gray's bestseller, *Men Are from Mars, Women Are from Venus*. But the reality of life and work is that men and women are similar *and* vastly different. We all stand to gain more by amplifying and leveraging those differences, which lead to greater contributions, than by continuing to minimize or ignore reality. Being equal is not the goal to strive for; valuing difference is the goal. And what is true for gender differences is also true for race, age, and other differences.

As humans, we all share similarities. Yet blacks are different from whites, older people are different from younger people, gender identity is not limited to male-female (but runs across a spectrum), gay people are different from straight people (another spectrum), and so on.

66 *Being equal is not the goal to strive for; valuing difference is the goal."*

To create and sustain diverse, inclusive workforces requires that we get our individual and collective logic and emotive systems working better together so that curiosity and wonder about difference replace fear, disdain, and hierarchies around who is better. This is hard, intentional work that strips away rhetoric and deals with root causes of discrimination. Those leaders who challenge themselves and their teams to do this will develop organizations that innovate and dramatically outperform others. Of equal

importance, they'll create humanistic environments where differences are valued and leveraged. The potential is enormous and exciting, but it's limited to brave leaders truly up to the challenge.

Examining Your Assumptions and Beliefs

What I think and how I feel about you says a lot more about me than it does about you. Think about this. Human beings are born with inherent programming that makes us suspicious of others who are different. Add to our biological programming the beliefs we hold, based on what we were taught as we were growing up, and the experiences we've had in our lives. All of this becomes the basis for many human actions. When we act on these influences (which we constantly do, until we raise them to a level of awareness), we sometimes find ourselves making decisions based on negative feelings of dislike or distrust, even if we often may not be able to articulate why we feel as we do.

> 66 *What I think and how I feel about you says a lot more about me than it does about you."*

In business, we say things like "Something about her just rubbed me the wrong way," and use these feelings as a basis for decision-making, when they could instead be used to signal discomfort that could actually be a hidden belief or assumption we never thought to question. Increasing the number of feelings allowed into our emotional ecosystems is extremely challenging. It is just so much easier to stay comfortably within our biases. But exposing ourselves to thinking or people that we perceive as different or that make us uncomfortable is also what inspires creativity in individuals and innovation in teams. We need to learn

to see the trigger of discomfort as a positive signal of differences among individuals.

66 *Exposing ourselves to thinking or people*
that we perceive as different or that make us
uncomfortable is also what inspires creativity
in individuals and innovation in teams."

When people begin to intentionally work to cultivate emotions appropriate to situations, then the possibility of bias enabling skewed decisions can be reduced. This holds profound opportunity in diverse recruitment, hiring, and total employee engagement. Being from a different race, gender, or ethnicity makes a person different, not deficient. A diverse company cannot develop and be sustained unless the individuals in the company have belief systems that work inclusively.

66 *Being from a different race, gender, or ethnicity*
makes a person different, not deficient."

Developing cultural curiosity by exploring and understanding the forces that underscore your beliefs and assumptions about yourself and others is a powerful replacement for judgment and bias. But this is learned behavior that leaders, managers, and workers need to be willing to develop. It does not, and will not ever, just happen naturally. Those organizational leaders who take the steps to acknowledge the real problem will position themselves to gain the tremendous advantages that come from having an equitable, inclusive, and diverse workforce. Yet, to do so will require self-reflection and fundamental changes to the way business and technology leaders think.

Quick Summary

Here are some key points to remember from this chapter:

- Fifty years of policy, law, regulations, and diversity and inclusion (D&I) initiatives have not addressed the real problem. The root causes of discrimination (bias) lie in our unstated, hidden beliefs.

- Self-development is leadership and employee development. A diverse company can't develop unless the leaders and individuals in the company have belief systems that work inclusively.

- The business case for diverse, inclusive workplaces is profoundly compelling but stifled by people's unwillingness to feel the need for change and to act on it.

- A business case alone is insufficient to develop a diverse and inclusive workforce, because organizational culture often limits the ability to execute on the business case.

- Differences in people are not deficiencies. Embracing difference requires us to experience and allow discomfort.

- Cultural curiosity is the most powerful replacement for judgment and bias.

Action Steps

Need to know how to apply what you just read? Here are some steps and ideas:

Continued

- Hire or appoint a senior-level chief diversity & inclusion officer (CDIO), who is a direct report to the chief executive officer (CEO). Qualities and characteristics to look for include:
    - A demonstrated success with building and delivering a comprehensive diversity and inclusion strategy with proven results.
    - A background in and experience with Organizational Development, Behavioral Psychology, Behavioral Economics, or similar.
    - A demonstrated ability to lead challenging conversations that are atypical in the workplace.
    - A willingness to experiment with new and different approaches to developing a diverse, equitable, inclusive workplace.
    - The ability to provide executive oversight of diversity programs, policies, and metrics to foster an environment of inclusion.
    - Well respected throughout the organization, with the ability to influence key stakeholders.
    - Fast-thinker and learner who is agile with change.
- Using the IAT, measure your board of directors to ensure diversity of bias.
    - The Implicit Association Test is available online at implicit.harvard.edu/implicit/takeatest.html.
    - Begin with testing for race, gender, and age biases.
- Measure the inclusiveness of the CEO as a leader. Develop accordingly, based on the results. Have the chief diversity & inclusion officer at your company act as or appoint an executive coach for the CEO, developing an actionable

plan with a timetable for results that can be later shared with the company's executive diversity committee.

- Calculate the cost of the status quo and develop your business case for D&I. Have the CDIO and CEO jointly present the business case to the board of directors. There are multiple ways to compute a business case, depending on the size, age, and other characteristics of the organization. Here are some steps to consider:
    - Analyze your current workplace demographics (EEO and other data typically found in HR systems).
    - Compute return on investment (ROI) of workplace D&I by linking EEO (demographic) data to business data (such as revenue or profits) through a correlation or regression analysis.
    - Set goals. For example, increase underrepresented minority female hires by 5% within six months.
    - Examine existing sourcing, recruiting, hiring, and retention practices and policies to identify hidden biases.
    - Demonstrate the ROI of enhanced workforce D&I by leveraging above linked data. Quantify effects, such as "For every 2% increase in racial diversity, the company experiences a 10% increase in inclusion, which drives a 20% increase in revenue."

- With support from multiple functional areas (i.e., Learning & Development, Leadership Development, and the D&I team), educate the board of directors and the entire organization on unconscious bias, developing cultural curiosity, and the power of self-reflection and beliefs. Leverage outside sources (training vendors and expert

Continued

consultants) if the company does not have the internal talent to do this work.

- Redesign the physical work environment to support differences. Changes such as screen savers; pictures and descriptions of female, Black, Latina, or other diverse business pioneers; paint color; music selection; and more provide subtle shifts that can bring about behavior changes that support inclusive differences among your workforce.

CHAPTER TWO

Reframing Your Thinking

We are all captives of culture.

—EDWARD T. HALL, PHD, ANTHROPOLOGIST

In spite of what we might like to believe, the culture of any given organization does not spontaneously or mysteriously develop. The founders of an organization instill their company culture with their values, beliefs, and assumptions. The learning experiences of the first employees—people who share the vision of the founders, believe in the mission, and are willing to assume the risks—also serve to inform the developing culture, but it's the founders who impact and influence culture the most. This first group of employees, led by the founders, effectively sets up the process of culture formation.

Informed by the vision and mission of company leaders, teams typically begin to seek funding, secure workspace, build products, develop services, and do the work that's needed to grow and manage a new company. As more people are hired, the history of the organization begins to take hold, and the vision and mission of the company's leaders become embedded in the values, beliefs, and assumptions of the founding group. Basically, at this point, they've established the corporate norms and the accepted way of doing things.

Looking at Your Organizational Culture

In sociology, a *norm* is known as an established standard of behavior, shared by members of a group, that each member of the group is expected to conform to. In business organizations, norms are informally taught to employees when leaders socialize the norms, act with confidence on them, and make decisions based on them.

Although company norms aren't documented as a part of the developing culture of a company, they are *profoundly* influential.[1] This is because the values embraced by an organization are implicitly governed by the norms of the founders; and as a result, employees are expected to act on those values.

As you think about how to develop, inform, or transform your organization, it's important to realize that fully effective leaders of an organization understand the business and human value of developing diverse and inclusive workforces. It wouldn't occur to these kinds of leaders to develop a company in any other way. Does your company have leaders who place value on a diverse and inclusive workforce? Have they set up norms in your company that support and sustain a culture of inclusion?

Building a Culture, Creating a Legacy

Kaiser Permanente (KP), one of the largest integrated healthcare systems in the United States, was founded in the early 1940s as the result of a collaboration between industrialist Henry J. Kaiser and physician Sydney Garfield. In its earliest beginnings, the Kaiser shipyards of World War II employed the first women to help build American ships in an industrial setting. By 1944, women accounted for 35% of the shipyard workforce. Kaiser next established the

first on-site, company-sponsored child-care centers in the United States, and then throughout the 1940s they hired an estimated 20,000 African-Americans, Chinese-Americans, Native Americans, and Latinos. In 1943, two decades before Civil Rights legislation was even passed, the Permanente Foundation Hospitals refused to discriminate, offering all its employees the same check-ups and quality of medical attention from KP doctors, regardless of gender or race. Even more, the KP public health plan took the lead in equal treatment of hospital patients in 1945, refusing to segregate them by color.

As the founders of KP, Kaiser and Garfield built an organizational culture that was progressive and innovative in the 1940s, showing that they not only valued diversity and inclusion but were also willing to take risks to make it happen. The corporate norms and organizational values of diversity and inclusion, embedded by the KP founders, continue to inform the award-winning culture of KP today.[2]

Inclusive Leaders

Truly inclusive leaders break from past norms, take risks, and champion a culture of diversity in their organizations. They don't make statements we sometimes hear people say, like "I'd hire them, but they're just not there," "It's going to take a long time to correct the diversity problem here," or "Changing the educational system is the real problem." They don't make excuses, shift responsibility to someone else, or shrink away because the work is hard. Inclusive leaders understand the essential value in diverse work environments and summon the courage to proceed toward that vision.

We're all learning how to establish diversity in the context of different workplace cultures, and sometimes this requires that we develop certain skills. But the goal is to have leaders in place who embody certain key qualities, whether they possess these qualities intuitively or they learn how to attain them. Inclusive leaders are people who:

- intentionally reflect on their beliefs and assumptions (which were instilled in them through the environments they grew up in, the people they interacted with, the values they learned from their families, and through their race, culture, and ethnicity);

- frequently examine their own unconscious biases and question the assumptions upon which they make major decisions;

- set highly aspirational targets for hiring and retaining diverse employees and hold themselves accountable to achieving these targets in specified timeframes;

- build inclusive practices into employee development programs and policies;

- acknowledge the traditional hiring practices and false beliefs about educational attainment, work experience, and social capital (relationship or network "connections") that have created the homogeneous companies that exist; and

- go where "they" are, knowing "they" are everywhere, and that contrary to popular belief, there is no shortage of qualified candidates, just a shortage of introspective and progressive thinkers.

DO YOU HAVE AN INCLUSIVE LEADER?

Want to find out if your leader is inclusive? Here are a few things you can do:

1. Start by asking a couple of simple but vitally important questions: Is your company leader trustworthy? Would customers, suppliers, and employees across organizational levels describe the leader this way? Trust is perhaps the single most pertinent characteristic of an inclusive leader because it is something that is earned, not given. Inclusive behaviors cannot be faked; even false pretenses of inclusivity reek with the smell of insincerity. If a leader acts with inclusive behaviors, that is someone who is typically trusted in a company.

2. You can also observe the actions and consistent behavior patterns of your leader. Is your leader genuinely open to input? Does this person respond to feedback from employee surveys, communicating that he or she has heard the workforce, is prepared to take action, and will share the results of those actions? These behaviors show that a leader is a person who cares about the differing perspectives of others, listens actively, and responds with action and transparency. Does your leader facilitate dialogue with curiosity and a desire to understand? These are traits and behaviors you want to see in an inclusive leader.

3. Take the test developed by the Catalyst organization to measure inclusive leadership. Here's the link: www.catalyst.org/knowledge/quiz-are-you-inclusive-leader.

Norms, Values, and Mental Models

Edgar Schein, former professor emeritus at the Sloan School of Management at the Massachusetts Institute of Technology, is a pioneer in the field of organizational development. For decades he's been widely recognized as one of the leading thinkers on the topic of organizational culture and leadership. He says organizational culture, which emanates from a company's founders, has three components. According to his definition, organizational cultures are built from:

1. artifacts, or what you experience with your senses (language, styles, stories, and published statements, like vision and mission placards);

2. espoused beliefs and values (ideals, goals, and aspirations); and

3. basic underlying beliefs (taken for granted and not questioned/discussed).[3]

Organizational culture is like the speed of light—it's impossible to change. When organizational leaders say, "We need to change the culture around here," what they're really saying is that they desire behavior change. Maybe they want managers to attend meetings on time or they want employees to be more customer-centric. These types of behaviors can often be altered by changing structure; leaders can introduce new policies or put reward systems in place, for example.

Other behavior changes, such as those needed to increase the amount of diverse talent in the organization, however, involve first identifying the underlying influences that reinforce existing behaviors. But becoming a more equitable, inclusive, and diverse organization requires a mindset shift that involves an intentional

movement away from being less self-conscious to becoming more interaction-conscious.

This is extraordinarily challenging, particularly for US-based companies, since this kind of mindset shift runs counter to the highly individualistic American culture. To change a company in this way asks us to go up against our accumulated learning, which is based on everything we've learned and experienced individually, in groups, and throughout a company up to that point.

Understanding the norms, values, and *mental models* (lenses through which each person sees the world) upon which the founders of your organization built your company is essential, since these directly affect the way people in the organization interact as well as the people who might even be asked to join the organization. As you think about bringing change to your organization, understand that organizational culture represents the collective values and beliefs of a larger group; it implicitly governs appropriate behavior for various situations, including how people behave toward others who are different from them.

To appreciate and understand the influences that strongly impact the leader(s) of your company, ask questions. Instead of asking about workplace issues or concerns, ask what life—not career—advice they would give to others or to you. Ask them what life advice they wish they had received themselves. Ask them about people who influenced them. Then you might begin to see the world and the company through the lens of the leader(s).

A Framework for Thinking about Differences

I once suggested to a group at a large, established organization that they should consider developing a separate leadership program just for women. One of the senior leaders of this company,

a white male, responded, "We don't need that. Sure, there are women who need help advancing in their careers, but there are plenty of men—including white men—who need help, too."

He was correct. But here is what he didn't acknowledge: an invisible structure exists in American society that operates to maintain the status quo. It is akin to hidden organizational norms; only in this case, we're talking about *societal* norms.

> " *An invisible structure exists in American society that operates to maintain the status quo.* "

Societal norms enable some people to move through life with ease and require others to work much harder to move forward. To be effective at developing diverse, inclusive work environments, we have to be willing to accept that this framework has influenced all of us—even people like me, who were taught to treat everyone with fairness and respect; even people who were raised in multicultural environments where they learned to embrace distinctions among people. Every person who is good-hearted, compassionate, and well-intentioned has still been shaped and influenced by the issues affecting equity, inclusion, and diversity. We are all complicit in keeping invisible forms of discrimination alive, regardless of our good intentions. The forces are invisible but powerful.

> " *Every person who is good-hearted, compassionate, and well-intentioned has still been shaped and influenced by the issues affecting equity, inclusion, and diversity.* "

To enable you to take a closer look at the ways in which issues of equity, inclusion, and diversity influence and inform the society in which we live and work, consider the following chart.[4]

Issues affecting diversity, equity, and inclusion	Variable	Accepted without question	Questioned with regularity
Racism	Race/ethnicity	White	People of color, non-whites
Sexism	Gender	Men	Women, gender-neutral
Homophobia/ heterosexism	Sexual orientation	Heterosexual	Lesbian, gay, bisexual, transgender, intersex
Religious oppression	Religion	Protestant	Muslim, Sikh, Jewish, Catholic
Classism	Socioeconomic class	Upper and middle class	Lower and poor working class
Elitism	Education level	College educated	Non-college educated
Militarism	Military status	WWI, WWII, Korean War	Vietnam, Gulf wars
Linguistic oppression	Language	English speakers	Non-English speakers
Ableism	Physical or mental ability	Able-bodied persons (body/mind)	People with physical, mental, or other disabilities

When we acknowledge that we have been shaped by the beliefs that enable the above framework, we position ourselves to become less defensive and more understanding of the opportunity to use this framework to guide meaningful dialogue about workforce effectiveness, diversity, and the sense of belonging that is inclusion. This is the beginning of becoming a more culturally effective person—and of understanding that a system of unearned advantage is a longtime structural institution that impacts our conscious and unconscious beliefs and behaviors.

As an example, prior to the Americans with Disabilities Act, not much thought was given to the challenge of entering a building or a bathroom in a wheelchair, because most people are able-bodied. The Disability Implicit Association Test shows that 76% of people have a hidden preference (bias) for able-bodied persons.[5] Similarly, the senior male leader mentioned earlier has never experienced the challenge of being female, since that has never been the lens through which he views the world. So this means that it's essential for each of us to understand our places in the framework of differences.

Those of us who go through life accepting things without question often behave in ways that assume what is true for us is also true for everyone. It takes humility to admit that some groups have it much easier than others based on variables none of us control. And it takes courage to act on this. Consider these scenarios:

- White men could be great allies to women in the workplace when they behave with a shared understanding that women are treated differently—and often more unfairly—than men at work.

- When a woman is interrupted in a meeting, a man could intervene, point out the interruption, and segue the discussion back so she could finish making her point.

- Men could campaign for onsite childcare, making this less of a women's issue.

- Able-bodied people could question the absence of people with disabilities in the workforce.

- Highly educated workers, committed to workplace diversity, could examine recruiting and hiring practices that favor upper socioeconomic classes.

When we choose to act, we use our privilege to make our workplace, society, and the world a better place for women, minorities, and other extraordinary people.

66 *When we choose to act, we use our privilege to make our workplace, society, and the world a better place for women, minorities, and other extraordinary people."*

In a study of *identical* resumes, one with a man's name and one with a woman's name, the study found that 79% of applicants with the man's name versus 49% of those with the woman's name were considered "worthy of hire."[6] This means that for all of us, reflection and deliberate intention are required in order to see systems as they truly are; until we do this, we won't be able to change them.

As we uncover our hidden biases, practice self-reflection, and grow in our curiosity about others, we can begin the process of writing what I call "mental prescriptions" to help keep ourselves in check. A feeling of discomfort in the company of people who are not like me is a normal feeling. When these instances occur, the mental prescription is a reminder that the sense of discomfort is about me, the person experiencing the uneasiness—not about the person(s) I am with.

Mental Prescriptions

Mental prescriptions are messages we create for ourselves to practice new ways of thinking—reframed thinking. When we think positively, we give others the benefit of the doubt. That is, we start from a place of assuming good, rather than bad, things about people or their actions.

Continued

When we're driving on the freeway and another person tailgates us, we may go negative and get annoyed, upset, or angry. We may think: "What's wrong with them? What's the big hurry? What a reckless driver!" and similar thoughts that typically run through a person's head.

Now, however, when someone tailgates me on the freeway, I try to move out of the way and let them pass. The mental prescriptions I write for myself say, "Perhaps they are nearsighted and overdue for an eye exam," or "They could be rushing their child to the emergency room." I try to come up with a thought that allows me to be sympathetic or amused, something that enables me to give this person the benefit of the doubt. The reality is that I don't know why they are driving so closely behind; they could in fact be reckless. But I can't control their actions. I can only control my response.

So how do mental prescriptions apply to workplace diversity? My friend and colleague Sam is a highly educated, accomplished African-American woman and corporate diversity strategist. She once facilitated a challenging discussion with a group of white men, trying to get them to own the privileges bestowed on them by society. She called me afterward to share her mistake in taking this approach and feared having done harm. When the men left the discussion that day, they were angry at the suggestion that they were somehow responsible for workplace discrimination and social injustice. Sam wrote herself a mental prescription. It said, "If I had entered the room giving the benefit of the doubt to those men—perhaps they are not even aware of systemic inequities—I may have had greater success in getting them on board to help fight inequality at work." Sam's truth is that she experiences daily

aggressions directed at her as a Black woman. But her anger at this injustice is about her, not about them.

Critical Thinking Takes Work

Learning to write mental prescriptions requires that we use critical-thinking skills. This means we need to be people who think for ourselves. We need to raise important questions, gather relevant information, think open-mindedly, and consider alternative views. We need to recognize and assess our assumptions and also consider both the practical and potential unintended consequences of these assumptions. Critical thinking is a skill set people develop with a lot of practice over time. We need to learn how to do this well if we ever want a chance at really changing the reality of hidden discrimination in our workplaces.

Individuals with a well-developed capacity for critical thinking possess what are sometimes called intellectual traits. This does not imply that an advanced degree is required to learn to think critically. To be clear, credentials have nothing to do with the ability to think critically. Anyone who is curious and has a desire to learn and to develop a stronger understanding of a topic can develop critical-thinking skills. Critical thinkers are people who act with courage, show empathy, possess humility, and are fair-minded. They have integrity and have mastered the ability to think for themselves. To develop these traits, they apply elements of reasoning. They ask questions and consider implications and assumptions. They evaluate the purpose of a discussion or topic and look at different viewpoints. Their reasoning is guided by a desire for clarity, precision, accuracy, and relevance. And they care about fairness and seek to understand issues beneath the surface.

I think of critical thinkers as people with enlightened traits. We are using critical thinking when we hear or see something and decide to suspend judgment so that we can check to see if it's valid; when we take multiple perspectives into consideration; when we consider the consequences of an action or the implications of things we believe; when we use evidence as a basis for decision-making; and when we reevaluate a viewpoint or belief in light of new information.

The three dimensions of critical thinking defined by the *Foundation for Critical Thinking* are shown as follows.[7]

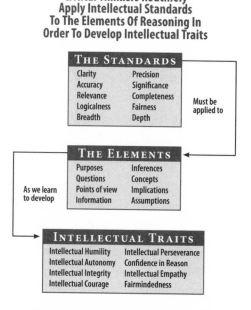

Critical Thinkers Routinely Apply Intellectual Standards To The Elements Of Reasoning In Order To Develop Intellectual Traits

THE STANDARDS		
Clarity	Precision	
Accuracy	Significance	Must be
Relevance	Completeness	applied to
Logicalness	Fairness	
Breadth	Depth	

	THE ELEMENTS	
	Purposes	Inferences
	Questions	Concepts
As we learn	Points of view	Implications
to develop	Information	Assumptions

INTELLECTUAL TRAITS	
Intellectual Humility	Intellectual Perseverance
Intellectual Autonomy	Confidence in Reason
Intellectual Integrity	Intellectual Empathy
Intellectual Courage	Fairmindedness

What does all this mean? As humans, we have the built-in tendency to believe things as we perceive them to be. We usually view ourselves as objective and feel pretty confident about our beliefs. We see our ideas as meaningful because we've always believed them to be true, we want them to be true, or it's in our interest for them to be true. This winds up being an egocentric kind of thinking that's largely done without any objective questioning. It's a natural thing we all do.

Similarly, in groups and societies we tend to position our norms, cultures, and even religions as more valuable than those of others. We act in the way we are expected to act, not questioning or considering differences among others. This is a socio-centric kind of thinking that's profoundly supported by mass media, particularly social media, and it constrains us to the viewpoints of our own society and groups. Like egocentrism, we also tend to do this naturally and innately.

All of us regularly engage in these two less-than-rational ways of thinking. And while being egocentric and socio-centric are natural conditions in human development, critical thinking works differently and occurs when we actively and intentionally develop our skills in it. Author and creative innovator Scott Berkun says there are two questions that should be asked wherever people gather—in schools, meeting places, cafes, and anyplace where thinking for oneself is advocated:

Why do we believe what we believe?

How do we know what we know?[8]

There are courses that teach the art of debating, and the best of these take learners far beyond the ability to form a position, present evidence, or respond to objections. Optimal learning and speaking skills come when we are required to defend the opposite

position, the one that runs counter to our true opinions or beliefs. It's healthy for us to consider not just our own views but also counter views. As well, when engaged in debate, Berkun suggests we try asking people:

Who, besides you, shares this opinion (or point of view)?

What are your major concerns, and what actions will you take to address them?

What would need to change for you to develop a completely different (opposite) opinion?[9]

If we want organizations that are multidimensional, inclusive of differing viewpoints, and fair to all, then we need to encourage people to think for themselves, reward open-mindedness, and act in ways to show that the rights and needs of every worker are equal to our own.[10] Critical thinking does not occur naturally; it must be taught, fostered, developed, and rewarded. This active cultivation combats irrational tendencies and activates the ability to write mental prescriptions in support of progressive, diverse workplaces that will drive future success. It also quite literally expands our brain-processing power.

REORGANIZING YOUR THINKING

Follow me on this. The brain's ability to reorganize itself by forming new neural connections is known as *neuroplasticity*. From the moment we arrive into the world, we begin developing a belief system. As newborn babies, since we lack a developed capacity for rational, logical deduction, our first beliefs are based on our experience of the world. As we grow and mature, our skills, knowledge, abilities, and understanding of the world expand. Our brains are constantly developing new and often stronger (based on length) neural connections, and in effect are reorganizing based on our new experiences.

Undertaking new experiences enables us to grow, learn, and effectively change the shape of our brains.[11] And new experiences enable us to push past the common binary categories we too often use—young and old, gay and straight, black and white. With gender, we assume people to be either male or female, thereby excluding individuals born intersexed (genitalia not definitively male or female). Exclusion minimizes people and makes them less visible. This then leads to them not getting the rights they deserve as humans. In politics, we focus on conservatives versus liberals and lose the value that independent, moderate views could bring to addressing national and global issues. New experiences provide the opportunity for us to reorganize our thinking, which betters us individually and the world collectively.

DISTINGUISHING CONSCIOUS FROM UNCONSCIOUS

The *reflective system,* or conscious mind, represents 10% of our brainpower, which thinks, plans, analyzes, and controls short-term memory. The *reflexive system,* or unconscious mind, represents the other 90% of our brainpower, including long-term memory, emotions and feelings, habits, relationship patterns, addictions, creativity, and intuition.

Our conscious mind takes certain actions, while our unconscious mind is the automatic system responsible for keeping us safe. When we're tired, stressed, frustrated, annoyed, or threatened, these emotions overtake our reflective control mechanisms, and our unconscious biases are triggered to take over our conscious behaviors.[12] This automatic triggering can be both helpful and hurtful. It's useful, for example, when I'm exhausted and working late in the office, and without conscious thought, to find something to eat or allow security personnel to walk me to my car. The times when automatic triggering might be hurtful to

me and others is when fear keeps me from engaging with others or taking action that could potentially benefit us.

Automatic triggering can prevent us from having the very experiences that may help our brains make new connections and grow. In these circumstances, mental prescriptions are useful, providing reminders that others may feel as uncertain about us as we do about them. Knowing this, we can take the first step and introduce ourselves.

PRACTICING MINDFULNESS

Mindfulness is a state in which we're intentionally conscious or aware of something. Recent work tying together neuroplasticity and mindfulness helps us understand how mindfulness can enable us to subdue our automatic responses so that we can be more thoughtful and flexible in our responses to others.[13]

For us, this insight holds profound possibilities. When we're intentionally mindful, we can seek to heighten our understanding of the beliefs and assumptions that drive people's behavior. We can also use mindfulness to learn new approaches to effective communications and decision-making in multicultural workplaces.

> 66 *When we're intentionally mindful, we can seek to heighten our understanding of the beliefs and assumptions that drive people's behavior. We can also use mindfulness to learn new approaches to effective communications and decision-making in multicultural workplaces."*

With the use of brain-imaging studies, the effect of thought on the brain, known as *self-directed neuroplasticity,* demonstrates that different types of mindful meditation actually bring about anatomical changes in the brain. We all sometimes operate

on "autopilot," when we eat something or drive somewhere or undertake some task based on habit and without real awareness of what we're doing. Mindfulness means not operating on auto-pilot. Instead, it requires that we pay attention purposefully and focus our attention on the present moment. When we're mindful, we maintain conscious awareness of our thoughts, feelings, and actions in a nonjudgmental fashion. We awaken to experience each moment as it is, and we value that experience.[14]

The book *Search Inside Yourself* offers three steps that are intended to allow people to change themselves in exceptionally short timeframes (from one day to seven weeks). The author, Chade-Meng Tan, an engineer, offers a course on this multiple times a year at Google, providing participants with hands-on practice with these three steps: attention training, self-knowledge and self-mastery, and creating useful mental habits.[15] Through the experiential course, people learn attention-focusing techniques to help bolster their creativity, reduce their stress, increase their empathy, and find ways to create greater meaning in their lives and jobs.

I think these same techniques could be leveraged for mindful meditation and reflection that would improve our brain neuroplasticity and help us become more compassionate to, and welcoming of, various types of persons.

By growing our self-awareness through mindfulness, we give ourselves permission to stop and consider our thoughts and feelings without judgment. The more we become aware, the easier it is to see where certain beliefs and actions might limit us. This self-compassion, which we all need in order to be able to look within ourselves and change those beliefs, also has the added benefit of expanding our humility toward others. We end up treating people different from us with greater kindness and caring.

Applying Evaluative Thinking

As we grow and mature, our experience of the world expands. The beliefs and assumptions that we develop in our lives are typically based on general methods of information gathering. We do this through:

- traditions perpetuated through our family ("We always cheer for the Red Sox!") or society ("Thanksgiving is an important holiday where I come from.")

- authority figures, like doctors who are considered experts in their field or teachers we look up to

- media messages and online networks that are designed to influence our beliefs

- our associations or who we hang out with (We often base our identities on our understood roles in a group, like family, work teams, or our community.)

- revelation (These, including gut feelings, intuition, premonition, or just a "sense" of something, are the most dangerous ways through which we gather information. When people say, "I just have a hunch," they're drawing on revelation. Revelation manifests at work when, for example, after an interview the evaluator says, "She's just not a fit here.")

Interestingly, only one method, evidence-based believing, stems from our ability to use critical thinking. The skills we associate with evidence-based beliefs are skills that develop over time through education. In a courtroom, evidence may show that one thing causes another, and understanding this appeals to people. It feels logical and makes sense. In business, education,

medicine, and many other fields, we typically look at events or outcomes that are measurable, scientifically studied, and tested with hypotheses.

But in actuality, the primordial power of our beliefs and assumptions comes far less from evidence. Family traditions and preferences strongly influence our religious practices, our political party preferences, and even our favorite sports teams. And society—through subtle and overt advertising, community groups, work teams, and our associates—also contributes to the informal information-gathering that profoundly affects what we believe and what we assume to be true.

What does it really mean to question assumptions in light of all this? It means that if we can apply evaluative thinking (also called critical thinking) to our life situations, it enables us to better consider varying points of view.

The Value in Questioning Assumptions

Throughout history, scientists have questioned the assumptions of others. Albert Einstein questioned Isaac Newton's widely accepted laws of motion. If he hadn't done this, he might not have gone on to develop his general theory of relativity.

On a more personal level, when my mother-in-law comes to visit, I never need to ask what time dinner should be served, because from her perspective, 5 p.m. is dinnertime. The assumption she makes is that people eat dinner at 5 p.m., and it does not occur to her to think about whether she is hungry at that time or not. She doesn't question it because it seems natural and normal to her. The rest of my family is not likely

Continued

to be hungry until later, so I find when I gently question her assumption, asking her if she's actually even hungry at 5 p.m., she pauses to think, considers a varying viewpoint, and typically adjusts the behavior around her assumption. This helps resolve a small family issue around dinnertime; and although it serves as only a simplistic example, it makes the point that there's often value in questioning assumptions.

In the workplace, assumptions that women are not as good as men when it comes to solving certain math or engineering problems can be a significant issue. Similarly, assumptions that whites have greater intellectual ability than Blacks, that younger people are more technically savvy than older people, or that men are better than women as CEOs of large companies (because they hold the majority of these positions) are assumptions worth questioning.

Beyond the workforce, there are also many more common stereotypes in parts of the world that are based on false assumptions. The idea that women are better than men at caring for children and elders, or that Blacks have more natural athletic ability than whites, are examples of assumptions that prove to be extremely limiting and problematic. As we surface our unconscious biases, questioning our beliefs about gender and family, Blacks and whites, and a host of other hidden preferences, we can empower ourselves to learn and grow by using evaluative thinking.

66 *As we surface our unconscious biases, questioning our beliefs about gender and family, Blacks and whites, and a host of other hidden preferences, we can empower ourselves to learn and grow by using evaluative thinking."*

Think about something you strongly believe. Ask: "Is this belief true?" "Is this belief serving me?" "What would happen if I chose to believe something else?" Challenge yourself to investigate this belief by using trustworthy, scholarly, objective sources. Just because all your friends on social media think something is true, or you heard it on a news report, doesn't mean it's based on verifiable evidence.

If we begin to question things we believe and hear, our investigatory powers can lead us to much greater learning. But we need to be willing to be wrong, to empathically put ourselves in the place of others, and to adopt new mindsets and beliefs based on evidence, not hearsay or misplaced trust in advertising or social media.

> " *We need to be willing to be wrong, to empathically put ourselves in the place of others, and to adopt new mindsets and beliefs based on evidence, not hearsay or misplaced trust.*"

Challenging Yourself

The unconscious belief that Blacks are inferior to whites is widespread, according to the data compiled from millions of people taking the Implicit Association Test. Yet, scientific evidence shows that there's no biological difference between races. Race is a social construct. But how often are your actions guided by implicit beliefs?

Challenge yourself by going to implicit.harvard.edu/implicit/ to see what group you're in: the 76% of people who unconsciously prefer white people over Black people, or the 24% who do not.

Anytime you question your assumptions and beliefs with a genuine desire to learn, you invite a level of discomfort. It takes openness, a willingness to be vulnerable, internal fortitude, and a lot of maturity. You'll also need to be able to do it with nonattachment. Questions you could begin to ask yourself include:

- "Do my beliefs have a solid basis and serve me well?"
- "Do I feel threatened when my beliefs seem to fall short or come under attack?"
- "Am I truly open to the views of others?"
- "Do I have biases or preferences that I need to examine?"

Deciding What to Do about Bias

The human brain is hardwired to be cautious about differences of all sorts. Each one of us is uniquely different, so our human tendency to congregate with others based on shared gender, race, ethnicity, skills, abilities, and interests is natural. Unconscious biases are, quite simply, preferences we are unaware of. Inherent mechanisms in human brains enable situations to be simplified so that we can process them automatically and quickly.

66 *Unconscious biases are simply preferences we are unaware of."*

If you are driving in traffic and a car suddenly veers in front of you, your brain acts without conscious thought and you step on the brake. Humans have evolved to be cautious about people, animals, things, and situations that are unfamiliar and, therefore, potentially unsafe. However, the same implicit assumptions may also lead us to make prejudicial judgments about people who are different from us.

Seeing through Our Biases

My friend Katy Wright has been teaching incarcerated prisoners for nearly a decade. She loves her work and the opportunity to help people who have a desire to better themselves actually be able to do so. Her courses include prescribed curricula from the penal system, but she's also taught communication skills to fathers behind bars so that they may maintain positive contact with their children while serving their terms.

Katy is limited in the kinds of questions she's allowed to ask the men, yet their stories emerge nonetheless. As pictures of each prisoner's upbringing, environment, and (frequently) horrific challenges they've faced emerge, along with the regrets they have and lessons they've learned, she develops a balanced empathy, a level of compassion, and an appreciation for each individual.

Not all of Katy's friends and acquaintances value her work. Some judge her, questioning why she might choose to "waste" her time teaching people who've committed crimes when the need for teachers in school systems is so great. Katy recognizes that the prisoners she helps are the kind of people others often try to avoid contact with. But she says that in her experience, the men who come across as the most intimidating in a dangerous system are typically kind, caring people and, surprisingly, some of her best learners. Her story teaches us that conscious and unconscious bias prevents many of us outside the system from ever seeing or even being open to the potential that lies within other people.

Scientific data about unconscious bias, implicit associations, and neuroscience clearly shows that we're *all* inherently biased. Like it or not, we are all somewhat racist, sexist, and a host of other unappealing labels. In fact, our biases typically run counter to what we believe to be true about ourselves. A stunning finding from the research on unconscious bias and implicit associations is that men are not the only ones biased against hiring and promoting women; women are often biased against other women; and Blacks can be biased against other Blacks.[16] So automatic are these preferences that we need to constantly self-evaluate our behaviors.

" *Our biases typically run counter to what we believe to be true about ourselves.* "

Recognizing that our biases can be at odds with what we think about ourselves will be a major challenge when we begin to deal with our unconscious biases. In our questioning and evaluating, we'll be confronted with the views we not only privately hold but also publicly state about the value and equality of people of all races, ethnicities, and other differences. It's not easy for any of us to see ways in which our demonstrated, measurable behaviors can be at odds with what we believe.

We use membership in social groups to make automatic, unconscious judgments based on how similar or different we are from others. This explains why we tend to socialize with others from the same socioeconomic class, age group, and background. While this behavior is normal and natural, in business it serves an unintended consequence, because managers and leaders tend to hire, mentor, promote, and work with those like themselves. Diverse groups do not develop from these actions and behaviors; homogeneous groups do.

Allowing Discomfort

Substantial research validates that exposure to others is the single best way to remove bias and appreciate differences among people.[17] Knowing this, and acknowledging my disdain for radical Islamists and my growing discomfort with seeing Muslims in my community, I challenged myself to visit the Islamic Cultural Center of Northern California. I shared my decision to visit the center with no one, and while driving to Oakland, where the center is based, I had two conversations going on in my head: I told myself I could just turn around and go home (the comfortable thing to do), or follow through with the visit (the uncomfortable thing to do). Not sure how it would go, I was hesitant to put myself out there, even though I knew it could be a positive first step.

I proceeded to the cultural center, and the visit was rewarding beyond measure. When I arrived, I was welcomed by a diverse, compassionate, caring group of Muslims. They shared artwork and literature to help me understand the kindness and value in their religion. The visit disarmed me. It affirmed my decision to welcome uncertainty and allow vulnerability. In facing my discomfort and bias and actually taking action, I opened myself up to be able to develop appreciation for others different from me. I was able to listen, to learn, and to grow.

The ramifications of change, based on this experience, have been positive for me in both attitude and behavior. Today, I'm more conscious of and intentional about expending the effort to welcome others in my community; I'm better able to act with compassion for people's circumstances and feel gratitude that they're here.

The next time you feel that someone different from you makes you uncomfortable simply because of that difference, consider taking a deep breath and recognizing this as a flag that you can react positively to. Work within your discomfort zone, acknowledge that the feeling you have is about you and not necessarily about them, and do the right thing. Give that person a chance to join your company, be promoted in your organization, take on a stretch assignment, and so on. Reflect. Be mindful. Use evaluative thinking skills.

Most reasonable people would agree that it's neither fair nor smart to select a CEO just because he's tall, or treat a patient with less compassion because she's overweight, or hire a person named John versus Jane or Jamal if all three have the exact same credentials and experience. Yet data shows us that this occurs with regularity.[18] Part of the reason is that our hidden biases enable these very occurrences.

If an inclusive leader does not want to limit human potential in an organization, this leader needs to work to recognize and counter the unconscious biases that drive these behaviors, and it must be a top organizational priority, not just for the recruiting staff, the people in human resources, or certain portions of the workforce. This must be a top priority for the chairman, the chief executive officer, all of his or her direct reports, all of *their* direct reports (Levels 1-2-3), and the board of directors, cascading down through the entire workforce. Taking one training class to learn about unconscious biases, while helpful, is grossly insufficient, because this is not a once-and-done undertaking.

Regular exposure to the Implicit Association Test (IAT) will help anyone who is interested in uncovering their hidden biases so that they can counter them. Most people who take the IAT (myself included) are unpleasantly surprised by evidence that shows their

actions are out of sync with their professed beliefs and intentions. While we like to believe we're progressively open-minded, fair, and without prejudice, it's of course unsettling to find out that the opposite is often true. We can console ourselves with the knowledge that this does not mean, however, that we are bad or immoral people.

Oftentimes we are not aware of bias that is innate, hardwired, or unconscious. However, when we challenge ourselves to become aware of possible bias, then we must decide what to do about it. Once bias rises to a level of conscious awareness, we have the opportunity to overcome the bias, with practice, and thus to change our thinking, ourselves, and our environment.

There's a big, looming question about whether company leaders and staff are willing to change their deeply rooted attitudes; and so feelings of shame, embarrassment, and disgust—both inside and outside the organization—may appear. Once we're educated about an important topic that we know has potential negative effects, we must change our actions, assuming we have the desire and skills to do so.

66 *When we challenge ourselves to become aware of possible bias, then we must decide what to do about it."*

Many companies, technology organizations in particular, insist they want a diverse and inclusive workforce. Yet data reveals that these companies are usually heavily male-oriented, mostly white, with some Asian and Indian employees; women, Blacks, Hispanics, and other minorities are severely underrepresented in these organizations. Exclusionary behaviors, resulting from unconscious negative biases, hidden beliefs, and even positive intentions that have negative unintended consequences, have led to the disparity in numbers.

To illustrate, let's talk for a moment about the widespread, implicit belief that older people don't understand technology as well as younger people. If teams that develop technology products in a company hold this implicit belief, or bias, they may likely refuse to solicit input from older people or value the suggestions of older people. This could prove to be a huge missed opportunity for a company to explore the thinking and ideas of a group with rich life experience, insights, and expertise to offer. And, given that the global population age sixty and over is projected to reach nearly 2 billion by 2050, this could mean the potential loss of a successful new product and services market.[19]

HOW BELIEFS AND ASSUMPTIONS
RELATE TO DIVERSITY AND INCLUSION

Invisible dimensions of thought are assumptions, values, and beliefs. Visible dimensions of thought manifest as behavior.

The cause-and-effect relationship is this: behavior is a direct result of what people assume, value, or believe. In other words, our thoughts are invisible to others and are based on what we value, believe, and assume; our actions are visible to others. So there's a relationship here—how we act is a result of what we think.

Ask yourself:

- What beliefs and assumptions have I formed about other people that are based on misconceptions?

- How has this caused me to exclude others?

- How may I act in the future to become more inclusive of people who are different from me?

Meritocracy Is a Myth

We've all heard it said that America is the "land of opportunity." Belief in the American Dream is about can-do individualism and goes something like this: anyone in this country can rise to a level of success based on his or her talents, abilities, and hard work. But children also inherit different starting points from the parents they were born to or raised by. Children from poor families have to work much harder to benefit from the privileges afforded the middle and upper classes. Social class, immigration status, and discrimination (conscious and unconscious) are factors that impede a fair and equal system of opportunity for all. And, of course, inherited wealth says *nothing* about the talent, ability, or hard work of the person inheriting the benefits.

Most companies want us to believe that they hire and promote the most-qualified applicants, regardless of gender, race, age, or other differences. Technology companies and select others claim that their overwhelmingly young, white male-dominated workforces simply reflect the larger problem of insufficient numbers of older people, Blacks, Latinos, or women available with the skills necessary to do the job. The sentiment is "We'd hire them, but they're just not there."

More recently, the tech industry has begun to acknowledge ways in which unconscious biases get in the way of hiring others who are not like people already in the industry. Even when the most-qualified applicants for a position are women or people from underrepresented minorities, the reality is that company leaders tend to still hire based on who they feel the most comfortable with—applicants they can relate to or who they think would be a good "fit" in the organization's culture.

For an industry that prides itself on daring innovation, the situation demonstrates stagnant, backward thinking that, even if

inadvertent, is designed to minimize diverse hires. Tech companies seem to want and favor underrepresented minorities who grew up in affluence, attended top-tier universities, and possess myriad connections to leverage—elitists, like them.

A System That's Rigged

Debby Irving, in her book *Waking Up White, and Finding Myself in the Story of Race,*[20] shares her feelings about discovering that the GI Bill, instituted at the end of WWII to help returning service people obtain higher education and secure home loans, was, through its implementation, effectively for whites only. At the time, a quota system limiting the number of Black students in colleges and universities restricted the number of eligible Blacks who could attend. Yet a preponderance of returning GIs, about one million, in fact, were Black.

At the same time, the Federal Housing Administration (FHA) hindered opportunities for non-whites to purchase homes by instituting policies suggesting that the skin color of a homeowner could affect the value of a given home in a neighborhood. This perpetuated a common belief that if Black people, or other non-whites, moved into white neighborhoods, housing values would decline. Specifically, the FHA gave builders loans through banks, on the condition that no Blacks could be sold homes in subdivisions. Also, no suburban homebuyer could resell to a Black person; and should this occur, the white neighbor could both evict the Black homeowner and be entitled under the law to collect damages. These were known as housing and neighborhood covenants.

Eventually, these practices were ruled illegal, and the Fair Housing Act contained in Civil Rights legislation during the late 1960s changed the law to remove discriminatory housing practices. But by

then, the damage was done. As a result of public policy, inner-city public housing became all Black, while suburbs became all white. Whites got equity appreciation from their housing, while Blacks did not, the effects of which continue to this day.[21] The bottom line is that many whites gained education and housing benefits during this time in history, but fewer than 5% of Blacks did.[22] The "American Dream" was rigged by a system of discrimination.

Many Americans acknowledge historical forms of discrimination, including mass killings of Native Americans and the displacement of the remaining Native Americans to reservations; Africans brought to America and sold at auction as slaves; Jim Crow legislation; and the internment of Japanese-Americans during WWII. Whites, the primary beneficiaries of opportunities during these times, can be labeled the "in-group." All others were considered the "out-groups." When we act as though the small number of women and minorities in technology and other industries is due to individual failings or lack of availability in the market, we elevate the idea of meritocracy and ignore the effects of hidden bias, subtle prejudice, and systemic discrimination.

66 *When we act as though the small number of women and minorities in technology and other industries is due to individual failings or lack of availability in the market, we elevate the idea of meritocracy and ignore the effects of hidden bias, subtle prejudice, and systemic discrimination."*

Laws have changed since the end of WWII, but to what extent have beliefs and behaviors changed? Do employment and promotional opportunities exist equally today in companies? Clearly not. Unconscious bias alone prevents that. The top jobs go primarily to white men, role models for women and minorities

are few, and opportunities for people who are a part of the "out-group" occur at an astoundingly slow pace.

Leave-of-absence policies, designed mainly for women with childcare and eldercare responsibilities, and performance evaluation systems that say more about the person giving the assessment than the individual receiving it, perpetuate discrimination under the guise of "helpfulness" or "merit."[23] We need to ask some tough questions about whom our systems and policies are really helping—and whom they leave out.

Perspective

Imagine a black person and a white person in a race together. The white person has a jet pack, and the black person does not. Both people run like that for a little while; then someone says that this isn't fair. So, the white person has the jet pack taken away. But the race doesn't start over; it just continues from where the runners were. A few minutes later, someone says that this still isn't fair, because although no one has a jet pack now, the white runner has already benefited from its earlier use. Since the race can't be started over, this person suggests giving the black person the jet pack for a little while.

In response to this, someone else asks, "But isn't it racist to give the jet pack to a runner, based on race?"[24]

This story illustrates the structural institution we're all born into and suggests that we're all complicit in perpetuating a system of bias. "Restarting the race" for blacks, Latinos, Native Americans, women, people with disabilities, individuals with non-heterosexual orientation, or those with other differences are not options.

Intervening

Interventions, however widely implemented, can serve to advance diversity in organizations. When some equally qualified candidates are competing for a job and the role is given to the underrepresented minority, this may be selection bias—but it is justified selection bias. The company wants and needs a diverse workforce, and the candidate deserves to "wear the jet pack" for a time.

Those leaders and teams progressive enough in their thinking to take this approach need to prepare for the inevitable backlash that will arise. The myth of meritocracy holds that the women and minorities selected with intention got their role only because of their minority status. This implication assumes that the person is not as qualified or credentialed as the individual who was not selected.

It's imperative for leaders to openly address that their decision to employ selection bias is from among *equally qualified candidates*. It takes courage and forward thinking to act on these important choices. And individuals, groups, organizations, and society benefit from this selection.

The myth of meritocracy is used inside and outside many sectors to justify the lack of diversity. It's essentially like telling women and underrepresented minorities that they only have themselves to blame if they didn't get the job or the promotion. And when women and people of color exit the workforce with much greater frequency than white, Asian, and Indian men, the self-serving belief in meritocracy lessens the need to address the issue and examine why this even happens.

Dismantling the myth of meritocracy makes us all accountable for racism, sexism, classism, elitism, and all the other *ism*s we've perpetuated on one another. Those companies who ground themselves in truth, data, introspection, and reality—for

instance, companies scoring high in the global *DiversityInc* Top 50 annual survey—are excellent examples of how to do the work of diversity and inclusion and succeed. Other organizations would do well to learn from them.

A Success Story

Sodexo, the 19th-largest employer in the world, with over fifty years of success, has 420,000 employees, comprising more than 100 different cultural backgrounds. Operating in eighty countries, Sodexo is the global leader in quality-of-life services, which support the well-being of people in their daily living, including in workplaces, schools, and healthcare settings. Its stellar work focuses on improvements to the environment, community health, and socioeconomic opportunity, all factors that affect the overall quality of human life.

What does this impressive company say is the reason for its success? According to Sodexo's 2016 employee survey, diversity and inclusion (D&I) is one of the top two drivers of worker engagement. Its 2016 Global Diversity and Inclusion Report details a decades-long actionable commitment to diversity and inclusion as a business strategy that produces a significant global competitive advantage. Sodexo challenges itself with programs to hold all employees accountable to its diversity commitments. Its research shows that Sodexo teams made up of 40 to 60% female managers, called gender-balanced teams, have measurably higher performance than unbalanced teams. Specifically, these teams have greater engagement, higher brand awareness, better client retention, and increased profit and growth over three consecutive years.

Changing the way we think about companies by looking at how employee belief systems and values affect an organization holds exciting possibilities for the future. As inclusive leaders and their followers apply a framework to think about differences among people and use critical thinking to guide them, better decisions are made that benefit everyone. Unconscious biases exist in all people, but they're malleable—this is important to remember. The opportunity to make the unconscious conscious, be mindful, and apply evaluative thinking is hard work. But this hard work positions us to fix the myth of meritocracy and create organizations that thrive with brilliance and performance.

Quick Summary

Here are some key points to remember from this chapter:

- Focus your efforts on *behavior* change in the workplace, not culture change.

- Inclusive leaders break from past norms, take risks, and champion diversity in their companies.

- Develop a critical attitude toward what you hear, read, or are told. Encourage your capacity to question!

- Learning the framework to think about differences among people empowers everyone to better navigate those differences. This is hard work, but the payoff is tremendous.

- Mental prescriptions are messages we create for ourselves to practice new ways of thinking—reframed thinking.

- Our brains never stop growing. New experiences create new neurons.

- Mindfulness and evaluative thinking are complementary practices.
- Challenge yourself to see past and work through your biases.
- Remember that meritocracy is a myth.

Action Steps

Need to know how to apply what you just read? Here are some steps and ideas:

- Reframing the way you think through practice, awareness, and intention leads to new possibilities to achieve success in workforce diversity and ultimately the success of the company. To begin to do this, reflect on these questions:
    - Why do I believe what I believe?
    - How do I know what I know?
    - What would need to change for me to hold a completely different viewpoint?

- Ask yourself: "How are diversity and inclusion affected by the values, beliefs, and assumptions of my company founders?" Understanding the real company culture requires answering this question.

- Acknowledge and understand the framework for thinking about differences (pp. 61) and how your life has been affected by it.

- Just as you know your strengths and personality type, learn your unconscious biases, so that your awareness can help counter them for more effective decision-making. As you do this, practice mindfulness. One way to get started is to take the Implicit Association Test (IAT) at implicit.harvard.edu/implicit/takeatest.html. Learn your biases and actively work to counter them. Then, retake the IAT six months later to see how you have changed!

- Diversity begins at the end of your comfort zone. Lean into discomfort. Start to see this feeling like a *positive*, even essential, thing as you learn how to navigate differences among people.

- Practice the use of critical (evaluative) thinking skills. Write mental prescriptions to shift your thinking about those who are different from you.

- Ask yourself whether your actions work to support or dismantle "in-groups." Do your behaviors include or exclude others? What will you do to change this?

- Become a cultural detective. Work every day to develop curiosity about difference. You can do this by visiting your local cultural centers to learn about other cultures and people. You can also do this simply by asking questions. Always be in learning mode.

Making a Plan Like No Other

Unless commitment is made,
there are only promises and hopes . . . but no plans.
—PETER DRUCKER

If you want to transform your current organization into one that is more diverse and inclusive, you need to boldly rethink how you recruit, hire, engage, and manage your employees. In the movie *Apollo 13*, NASA Command Center engineers were tasked with saving the lives of three men stuck in outer space. They had to figure out a way, using only the materials on board the spacecraft, to lower the rising levels of CO_2 within the lunar module. This literally required fitting a square peg into a round hole. And they succeeded.

Creative Recruitment, Hiring, and Engagement

Changing a company into one that is diverse and inclusive is like fitting a square peg into a round hole. It takes a significant systemic change that can't be accomplished simply through a suite-of-diversity-initiatives approach. We can't depend on systems that

are already in place, since most corporate systems and policies have been designed around the myth of meritocracy. The existing systems around us don't account for unconscious bias, and hidden biases in companies just feed into the false idea of meritocracy.

We have to help organizations become deliberate, intentional, and unyielding about seeking out and valuing those who see life through a different lens—Blacks, LGBTI people, older people, the disabled, Latinos, females, Native Americans, Asian-Americans, and others. In the hiring process, for example, do you offer rewards to employees who recommend the candidates who later wind up getting the job? Since we know people tend to recommend new hires who look, sound, and think like they do, companies could reengineer the search process to offer rewards to those who bring in diverse talent. After all, isn't it imperative for us to examine all systems and processes in a company if we're to succeed in the D&I space?

This chapter will show you new work processes to attain desired outcomes, such as how to redesign performance management, measure and improve inclusive leadership, build cultural curiosity, interview holistically, and embrace humility. You'll learn how to find creative ways to recruit, hire, and engage a diverse and inclusive workforce, changing the landscape of companies, meaningfully impacting the way we do business, and transforming the entire current system to position your organization for success well into the future.

Finding the Right Talent

More often than not, the attitude toward hiring for diversity and inclusion seems to be "I'd hire them, but they're just not out there," or "I can't find them." (Never mind that referring

to someone as a "them" is problematic in and of itself, setting anyone who's different from us immediately in the position of the "other.") Even hiring managers in companies with stated workforce diversity goals and targets can have this kind of mindset. Add to this that people often say there's a "war on talent," reflecting the perception that even though the demand for specialized skill sets is high, the pool of qualified applicants is small; this is proven false when unemployment rates rise and a labor surplus is created, yet companies continue to struggle with the supposed problem of finding enough qualified applicants for a position.

Today we not only have the power of automation to help minimize bias but also can use big data to seek out candidates. Entelo, an online platform, makes it possible to build more diverse candidate pools while reducing the time to hire. Software tools like Textio let us leverage machine learning to compose better job descriptions that lead to hiring more diverse talent pools. And GapJumpers takes an approach to diverse talent selection by using blind auditions, in which names, cities, and other identifying criteria are hidden from interviewers to enable them to find untapped talent without bias or other influencing factors.

Yet in spite of technological advances to help us in our hiring, companies claim there are still just not enough qualified candidates to be found. Really? When I talk with employers through the work I do, I'm told there are more people to hire, just not more people with the right skills. Are we certain about this? Have we clearly defined what the "right" skills are? Or, is this a cover for a very different problem? Are the companies that are lamenting about so-called talent shortages merely presenting themselves as victims of a problem they've inadvertently helped create?

No Lack of Talent

In 2016, I attended the PUSHTech2020 Summit, part of an initiative of the Rainbow PUSH Coalition to call on technology and telecommunications companies, particularly industry leaders in the Silicon Valley, to be truly inclusive in their employment policies and practices. The summit, held in San Francisco, brought together Rev. Jesse Jackson, members of the Rainbow PUSH Coalition, entrepreneurs, and established technology company leaders. Diversity and inclusion champions from Yelp, Dropbox, Pinterest, Airbnb, Twitter, Intuit, Solar City, and many more companies attended, along with investors from Fairview Capital, Kapor Capital, Intel Capital, and Google Ventures. These are companies that recognized the problems arising from a lack of diversity in workforces, among top senior executives, and on boards of directors in key business sectors.

During a keynote speech, a room packed with hundreds of people burst into applause when Brian Krzanich, CEO of Intel Corporation, boldly pronounced, "There is no pipeline problem." He said that the issues with diversity recruitment and hiring are not due to a lack of talent and that companies claiming otherwise are only making excuses.

It was validating and reassuring to me, and to the many others who attended the summit that day, to finally be able to hear an influential leader of a major company share his discovery and acknowledge the state of things. This was an important truth, given to us from the real-life experience of a major power player in the industry.

BUILDING UP THE WORKFORCES WE HAVE

Since 1990, the number of US workers receiving employer-sponsored training and education has been in decline, with a dramatically steep drop to 42% around 2008.[1] If employers today were willing to pay high wages for skilled talent, but the demand for ready-made talent was in fact larger than the supply, then why wouldn't a company stop "buying" new talent through high wages and instead begin to "build" talent from internal pools instead? Yet we see companies continuing to pursue new candidates, following the same practices of recruiting, seeking the same profile types they're accustomed to hiring, finding the same talent that keeps their workplaces homogeneous.

If the technical skills needed in the workplace change so rapidly that only the most premier of universities can act as feeder pools to companies, but somehow this still doesn't seem to produce enough students to be able to fill the demand, how does it make sense for firms not to develop talent internally? Shouldn't companies invest in training and developing the workforces already available to them?

The counterargument to this, of course, is often "What if we invest in training them, only to have them later leave?" While there's some validity to this, the data has shown for decades that people leave employers largely because of poor relationships with managers, lack of challenging work, unsatisfactory work-life balance, or other life events. It just makes sense intuitively that employees who work in positive, inclusive, dynamic environments, and under the leadership of managers who value their contributions, would be the people least likely to want to leave.

While today's companies might offer perks, like foosball tables, nap stations, and free food, the things that show employees they're truly valued are healthy work environments where

people are challenged, praised, encouraged, taught, listened to, and appreciated.

66 *Companies should invest in developing their existing talent pools so that vital work is produced by people rewarded by challenge in a company that believes in them."*

Companies should invest in developing their existing talent pools so that vital work is produced by people rewarded by challenge in a company that believes in them. It's fine to supplement internal talent with external hiring, but it's nonsensical to do it at the risk of losing other experienced performers. It's better to address the reasons why good people voluntarily leave and correct those issues, while also providing exciting opportunities to grow the talent you already possess.

LOOKING FOR GOOD CANDIDATES

When you need to look outside your organization for good, qualified candidates to fill roles in your company, think strategically about where you look and whom you open your search up to. It takes intentionality to not only build up but also develop a talented, diverse, inclusive workforce. You want to hire the best people, but make sure you're recruiting from all the right places, including places where you might not have looked in the past. Well-qualified candidates are everywhere; and if you're hiring for a particular industry, consider who might often be overlooked in that arena.

In the technology sector, we're seeing astounding growth trends with the number of undergraduate students majoring in computer science, computer engineering, and information degree production. The overall number of students in PhD computing programs has also reached a record high, and this is in

North America alone. With the rise in the total number of qualified college graduates that companies can choose to hire from, the
numbers of both women and minorities graduating from these
programs are substantial. Research shows that even as far back as
2012, the number of computing degrees awarded to women was
2,078 and the number awarded to minorities was 4,127.[2]

Like other universities, historically Black colleges and universities (HBCUs) offer technology-related degrees. Specifically, of
the total 106 HBCUs in the United States, 36 schools offer science, technology, engineering, and math (STEM) programs, and
27 schools offer master's and doctoral degrees in computer science, engineering, mathematics, or business.[3] While HBCUs are
not exclusively Black, they all offer a diverse talent base among
their student populations. Companies often look to hire from
the same large universities around the United States; but I'd say
there are likely a lot of qualified graduates and strong candidates
to pursue from HBCUs. Consider expanding your recruiting
to include different colleges and universities, not limiting your
choices to students from select schools.

Brand-name colleges are believed to produce the most intelligent talent, and students who attend these schools typically have
high IQs and test scores. Studies have determined that while IQ is
a predictor of high SAT scores, those SAT scores are not predictive
of either job performance or success in life.[4] Google, to its credit,
has analyzed this and publicly shared its findings that grade point
averages, test scores, and even college attendance are not indicators
of whether a person will be a valuable employee. Yet, a majority
of well-known, elite technology, consulting, legal, and investment
banking companies continue to operate by hiring almost exclusively from top-tier colleges and universities. And studies are clear
that the majority of students attending these elite schools come

from wealthy families with high socioeconomic status and have significant relationships they can leverage to help them succeed.[5] In other words, they come from homogeneous groups.

Innovative approaches to identifying needed talent should include looking at graduates of coding academies or individuals earning certificates of completion from select courses at some of the massive open online courses (MOOCs), many produced by MIT, Harvard, Stanford, and other highly selective universities. Is an academic degree a requirement for certain jobs or a myth we tell ourselves so often we believe it to be true? For some jobs, maybe it makes sense to eliminate the assumed need for a college credential at all.

There are extraordinarily successful people who either never attended college or dropped out. Ruth Handler, the co-founder of Mattel, observed her young daughter, Barbara, playing with paper dolls and went on to create her company's signature product— the Barbie doll. Literary genius Maya Angelou and international journalist Lisa Ling are two other examples. Bill Gates, Larry Ellison, Muriel Siebert (the first woman to purchase a seat on the New York Stock Exchange), and the late Steve Jobs (just to name a few) are all high school graduates who succeeded in their fields, absent college degrees. A desire to think more creatively and implement new techniques to finding diverse candidates can unearth phenomenal talent pools.

How else could companies find diverse talent? They could actively participate in any number of the thousands of professional associations for women, Blacks, Latinos, former military personnel, persons with disabilities, LGBTI individuals, and so on. Do you have an accounting or finance role to fill? Consider hiring through the National Association of Black Accountants (nabainc.org). More than 10,000 women skilled in technology

come together in celebration and learning at the annual Grace Hopper Celebration (ghc.anitab.org). Recruit there.

What else?

- Sponsor a Year Up (yearup.org) program in a low-income area near your headquarters. This program, seeking to close the opportunity divide, provides urban young adults with skills and support to empower them to achieve success through higher education and professional careers. You'll find innovative, resourceful people who have breadth and diversity of experience to offer.

- Help advance the I Love Being Black (ilovebeingblack.com) social media campaign and recruit from there.

- Collaborate with girlsteachinggirlstocode.org, in which Stanford women teach girls from the San Francisco Bay Area how to code, or with girlswhocode.com, a national nonprofit launched in 2012.

- Become involved with AnitaB.org, a nonprofit social enterprise that builds up women in computing by supporting women in technical fields, the organizations that employ them, and the academic institutions that train them.

- Check out Hire America's Heroes (hireamericasheroes.org), an excellent program for finding talent with military experience. Many veterans are skilled leaders.

- Follow the lead of companies like Northrop Grumman, Starbucks, AT&T, and Ernst & Young, who have attained top rankings on the US Business Leadership Network's (USBLN) Disability Equality Index (DEI) for successful and sustained hiring of people with disabilities.

- Inquire about supporting the expansion of CODE2040 (code2040.org), a program that mentors minority students and matches them to internships in high-tech firms.

Get wildly creative about how and where you might find new talent. Forget about thinking outside the box and ask yourself instead: Why is there even a box to begin with? This is where you start to push through past norms and conventions. This is where you think about what matters—for your company, for people, for society.

If you want to find good candidates for a diverse, inclusive workforce, go where they are. Meet the teachers and try to identify the students who are intrigued by the type of work you offer—and the promises the future holds. Work within local communities: offer internships, externships, on-site visits, innovative programs, and opportunities. Why limit your choices only to those who come to you? If you want to succeed, you must go out. And if your candidates come from a source that is not your standard top-tier feeder school, then recognize the diversity of experience you get by hiring them into the company.

Due to the increasing pace of change in business and the necessity of constant learning, all of your employees, at some point, will need some kind of ongoing development. You'll derive a lot of benefit from building (versus just buying) great talent, and this talent will also bring the diversity that the top schools cannot always deliver on. It's a classic win-win-win—for you, for the employees you hire, and for innovation from diversity.

The Most Diverse Counties in the United States

If your company is seeking to hire for greater diversity among ethnicities, the work of Randy Olson, a PhD candidate in Michigan State University's Computer Science program, might help you concentrate your efforts. Olson produced a visualization map of the United States that shows the distribution of ethnic diversity by county. Check out his work. Here also are the top five most racially diverse counties in the United States (and note that two of the top five happen to be within driving distance of Silicon Valley):[6]

1. Aleutians West Census Area, Alaska
   a. 31.4% White (non-Latino)
   b. 5.7% African-American
   c. 15.1% Native American
   d. 28.3% Asian-American
   e. 13.1% Latino
   f. 6.4% Other

2. Aleutians East Borough, Alaska
   a. 13.5% White (non-Latino)
   b. 6.7% African-American
   c. 27.7% Native American
   d. 35.4% Asian-American
   e. 12.3% Latino
   f. 4.4% Other

3. Queens County, New York
   a. 27.6% White (non-Latino)
   b. 17.7% African-American
   c. 0.3% Native American

Continued

      d. 22.8% Asian-American

      e. 27.5% Latino

      f. 4% Other

4. Alameda County, California

      a. 34.1% White (non-Latino)

      b. 12.2% African-American

      c. 0.3% Native American

      d. 25.9% Asian-American

      e. 22.5% Latino

      f. 5.1% Other

5. Solano County, California

      a. 40.8% White (non-Latino)

      b. 14.2% African-American

      c. 0.5% Native American

      d. 14.3% Asian-American

      e. 24% Latino

      f. 6.2% Other

RECRUITING FOR DIVERSITY OF THOUGHT AND EXPERIENCE

Many organizations will say that their #1 hiring criterion is basic cognitive ability—how well someone thinks, reasons, learns, and remembers. And some companies say that they value fluid intelligence, which is the ability to reason quickly and think abstractly, especially when dealing with complex information, more than they value crystallized intelligence, which involves the culmination of learning, knowledge, and skills acquired over a lifetime. This is basically a coy way of saying that they prefer to hire younger people, not older people.

But how is basic cognitive ability assessed in these companies? Isn't this almost comparable to the situation of higher-education entrance exams? The problem with hiring for fluid intelligence over crystallized intelligence is that it once again perpetuates a system that hires for sameness, not difference. It's another homogeneous process, especially since fluid intelligence tends to decline during late adulthood, when crystallized intelligence increases. Inclusive organizations value both and can drive greater performance because they have multiple generations in the workplace. It's called diversity of thought and experience.

While any employer would want to hire intelligent people, I need to point out that "G," which is the general measure of intelligence, and standardized IQ tests both have well-documented racial, gender, and cultural biases built in.[7] And compelling theories about human intelligence, such as those explained to us by Howard Gardner, the Hobbs Professor of Cognition and Education at the Harvard Graduate School of Education, challenge us to consider the many forms that intelligence actually takes. If we'd given a standard IQ test (which measures logical, mathematical, and linear thinking) to Beethoven and Mozart, they might have scored pretty poorly; yet we could probably make a pretty good argument that both composers are geniuses who innovated and contributed a great deal to culture and society.

66 *When it comes to whom we choose to join our ranks, let's get rid of the 'us versus them' kind of thinking in our companies and in the way we do business. Let's realize that the personal, business, and social value of blending new hires, who have both earned and unearned privilege, leads to powerful performance. And this benefits us all."*

Above all, when it comes to whom we choose to join our ranks, let's get rid of the "us versus them" kind of thinking in our companies and in the way we do business. Let's realize that the personal, business, and social value of blending new hires, who have both earned and unearned privilege, leads to powerful performance. And this benefits us all. Know that the talent you're looking for can be found because the talent is everywhere. You just have to look.

Enhancing the Hiring Process

For legal reasons, most job descriptions from US-based companies contain well-intentioned but misguided words that read something like this:

> *Employment by [insert name of company] is based on merit, qualifications, and competence. Applicants will not be discriminated against on the basis of race, color, religion, sex, gender identity, national origin, age, physical or mental disability, veteran status, sexual orientation, or any other status protected by applicable federal, state, or local laws.*

These words are hinged upon the idea that recruiters, hiring managers, and other people involved in the process of selecting new employees will not see color or disability, will not discriminate based on age or gender, and will make fair, objective, unbiased hiring decisions. In fact, companies will insist that they only hire the best person for the job and that their decisions are based on merit, skill, and ability. But how, exactly, is "best" even really measured or determined? *Subjectively.* That's how.

Substantial research on how unconscious biases affect our

actions confirms that our perception of "color-blindness," "gender-blindness," or "age-blindness" is actually blatantly false.[8] The typical interviewing process today calls for job applicants to convince an interviewer that they're a good "fit" for the organization. In this process, the onus is on job applicants to address unspoken biases and convince the interviewer about their values of leadership and dependability, and their skills, ability, and desire to do the work. But in the kind of process that should be our goal, the onus should also be on the interviewer to discover differences in the applicant as a means of adding to the diversity of the workforce. This can only occur, however, if inclusion is a core, embedded value in the organization.

Preventing Interviewer Bias

In 1970, women made up only 20% of all new hires by America's major symphony orchestras. Many people didn't believe that women had the lung capacity to play large wind instruments. Today, most symphonies hold blind auditions with potential candidates performing behind a screen so that judging panels can better make unbiased assessments based on the quality of playing. Since blind auditions began, the proportion of women hired by major symphony orchestras has *doubled*, from 20% to 40%.[9]

Businesses would do well to model this approach with their hiring practices. Interviewers could, for example, create environments—like pods—so that applicants cannot readily be seen; interviewers could use voice synthesizers to keep gender or ethnicity hidden. Finding creative ways to control

Continued

interviewing conditions, essentially holding blind auditions, could help prevent bias in hiring decisions.

At companies such as Blendoor, an inclusive recruiting and people analytics software firm, names, photos, and dates of job applicants are hidden on resumes specifically to mitigate unconscious bias in hiring and to accelerate the identification of qualified candidates. Organizations truly committed to diversity take action and leverage services like these. Imagine if the proportion of talented, qualified people we hired doubled the diversity in our workforces.

Large firms that receive hundreds or even thousands of job applications each day commonly use so-called predictive analytics to cull through large amounts of data and identify candidates for roles. To develop a multifaceted workforce, we need to understand the impact of these tools. Was a diverse group included in the development of the tools? What analytics does a particular tool predict? Are our hiring criteria truly fair?

If we examined the success of our current talent base, we'd find data only about our homogeneous workforce. And data we might have, like SAT scores or IQs, is not even correlated with a person's ability to be successful in a job. Where is the data on measuring different populations? The hiring criteria companies continue to use today have not worked to sufficiently develop teams that include women, African-Americans, Latinos, or disabled people—in other words, anyone who isn't young, male, and either white, Asian, or Indian. The use of nontraditional solutions to recruiting, hiring, and retention is *absolutely essential* if we are to be able to succeed in developing a diverse workforce.

In the sections that follow, we'll explore ways of rethinking, overhauling, and enhancing our hiring processes.

PRACTICING HOLISTIC HIRING

I worked for five years in a large San Francisco–based hospital system where I was responsible for continually and strategically improving the experience of patients and families. I saw first-hand the ways in which the recruitment and hiring of physicians focused primarily on their expertise and clinical excellence, which of course is essential to the practice of medicine and a skill set patients would understandably expect from their doctors. But I also observed that what patients wanted and what made a huge difference to them were the qualities of empathy, compassion, and genuine human kindness in their doctors.

Over time, I cultivated this thinking and began to speak at physician education sessions about the importance of what I called "hiring for nice." This recognizes that although empathy, compassion, and human kindness are not traits you can easily train into a grown person, you can do something about this and continue to bring in the best doctors for your patients. We developed behavioral-based interview questions to ensure that we were hiring for both outstanding clinical abilities *and* a genuine, caring nature. We began to ask interviewees questions like "Could you provide two examples from the past month that demonstrate how you showed empathy to patients?" and "What is the most emotionally stressful patient situation you have experienced? How did you show compassion to yourself and to the patient?" After we implemented this and other changes, we were excited to see that patient satisfaction scores rose for four consecutive years.

The business community could learn a lot from the medical community. After decades of stagnation when the primary—practically the sole—criterion for hiring physicians consisted of finding candidates who had excellent clinical competence, things began to change in 2008, when patient satisfaction scores became publicly reported. As in my experience, it became clear to healthcare professionals that patients valued physician compassion and understanding as much as, if not more than, a physician's clinical competence (which was automatically assumed).

The healthcare industry underwent a transformation, and even the entrance exam for medical school, known as the MCAT (Medical College Admission Test), was revised in April 2015 to include multiple questions designed to determine the depth of empathy in a prospective physician. In professional settings, interviewers began to consider more factors than just clinical expertise when they evaluated applicants. This movement toward *holistic hiring,* in which interviewers look specifically for nontraditional traits in their candidates, has both improved the quality of the physicians hired and also enhanced patient outcomes.

Think about qualities and characteristics—nontraditional strengths—you would ideally want to see in your workforce. Find ways to evaluate your candidates for these strengths. Create a framework for recruiting and hiring new people that's holistic in approach. Knowledge, skills, and abilities (KSAs) certainly matter in hiring, but the kind of person the candidate is matters even more. Unusual questions such as "Tell me about the last three books you read" and "Would the people who know you well describe you as empathic, sympathetic, or compassionate? Why?" will help deepen your perspective. The goal here is not to judge, but to gain insights into the *whole* person beyond the standard KSAs.

ASKING GOOD INTERVIEW QUESTIONS

We talked about holistic hiring in the medical community. What might holistic hiring look like in other industries or for other companies that want to create a diverse, inclusive workforce? Let's explore this using the technology industry as an example.

Technology companies often hire for math, computing, coding, and other specialized talents. They commonly use interview questions that test for an applicant's cognitive ability and adeptness at structured, logical thinking. But the questions they ask could also provide a larger, more holistic view of who the applicant is. When we interview, have we designed and included questions that allow us to see if candidates are empathic, culturally competent, and able to connect with others in ways that stimulate people's innovative thinking and ideas?

The questions may sound difficult to create, but consider these:

- "Give me an example of a time when, in spite of great pressure, you didn't go along with a group decision at work. How did you feel? Did others accept your choice?"
- "What is more important to you: Valuing differences among people or valuing commonalities among people? Why?"
- "Tell me about a time when you had to manage conflict in a multicultural group."
- "How comfortable would you be reporting to someone of a different race or gender?"
- "Give me an example of how you show respect to women at work."

Think about what kind of organization you're trying to create and the characteristics and emotional competence you want

employees to have. Then, experiment with a variety of behavioral-based interviewing questions until you land on a set that works well for your company. There is no formula for designing good questions to ask applicants, except perhaps to experiment, learn, and continually improve. Also, of course, stay within legal limitations with your questions.

Devising *and* asking good interview questions not only takes work and preparation but also requires courage. Be prepared for surprised looks or even negative reactions. We are, in a sense, rocking the boat and changing what people are accustomed to. But the downside of asking the same questions we've always asked in interviews is that our hiring practices perpetuate the same homogeneous workforces and environments that have held our companies back and kept us from working in wiser ways.

In tech jobs, are the same testosterone-fueled, adolescent, so-called brogrammer behaviors that get unleashed during the interview processes what we hope to have and advance in our organizations? There's a saying that goes "What we permit, we promote." If we rethink the way we interview and ask more thoughtful questions, we can transform our hiring practices for the benefit of all.

RESHAPING OUR THINKING ABOUT HIRING

During the hiring process, organizational leaders must model and communicate expectations for mutual respect and appreciation to people both outside and inside the company. They need to send the message that they are leaders who hold workers accountable for fostering an environment of acceptance and understanding. Internally, they need to also address the issue of employees who lament that bringing in diverse hires means "lowering the bar" or choosing someone "lesser" for the company.

The misguided perception that hiring women, people of color,

military, disabled people, or other applicants of different back-grounds is a charitable act smacks of prejudice that ultimately retards innovative progress. Leaders need to be able to read their employees and skillfully direct people toward an inclusive work-place culture.

One thing leaders and hiring managers can do is model something called *appreciative inquiry (AI)*, which is an approach to managing change that focuses on identifying what works well in a company and then doing more of it, as compared to focusing on problem-solving. Think of it this way: the traditional approach to hiring requires solving the problem of finding X number of people with the requisite skills and abilities to fill X number of roles. Searching for these people is tedious and time-consuming, and hiring managers often need to spend a lot of time weeding out candidates that are not a "match," just to get the applicant pool down to a more manageable size.

But suppose hiring was an enjoyable and productive process that we felt really good about. What if we've decided to hire holistically, looking at the whole person and not just his/her skills? What if we've designed interview questions to surface a candidate's strength of character? Appreciative inquiry is a tool to help you implement these changes. It's a creative, positive approach to hiring, and it's yet another way to help reframe our thinking about our organization's approach to diversity and inclusion.

Janet Cottrell, Senior Director of Academic Resources and an associate of the Center for Appreciative Inquiry at Champlain College, lays out an iterative approach to hiring using AI:

- Beyond the traditional knowledge, skills, and abilities (KSAs), identify what *key values* are essential for the job. Ask, "How do our company's values match up with this

candidate's values?" and "How might our comp...
evolve if this candidate joined the team?"

- Adjust your thinking about the searc...
eliminating candidates from the la...
the pool for as long as possible. ...
learn about this candidate?" ...
date bring to the team?"

- Seek success with ...
though you wa...
we showcase ...
and "Wh...
candidat...

What's the bottom ...
inquiry approach to hiring, ...
their thinking from looking at ...
instead noticing all the assets a cand...
more about a full process for using appr...
from the David L. Cooperrider Center for ...
visit the *AICommons* at https://appreciativeinq...
edu/wp-content/uploads/2017/10/Appreciative-Inq...
-recruitment-and-hiring-of-new-employees.pdf.)

As we formulate a new plan for hiring talent, we shoul...
aware of the false presumption that there is an actual, objective,
predefined bar against which we can measure candidates. The hiring process is dramatically more subjective than scientific. We
know that interviewees are rejected all the time for simply not
seeming like they'd be a great fit for a company's culture. But a
candidate declined by one company often makes an excellent hire
for another. The so-called bar and who clears it actually says more

---

- the ability to connect to others in a deep and direct way,
to sense and stimulate reactions and desired interactions
- proficiency at thinking and coming up with solutions and
responses beyond those that are rote or rule-based
- the ability to operate in different cultural settings
- the ability to work productively, drive engagement, and
demonstrate presence as a member of a virtual team

(See appendix two in the back of the book for a more comprehensive list of skills, as identified in the *Future Work Skills 2020* report.)

We need to be clear about the values we're hiring for and
not operate on the assumption that special skills reign supreme.
Some candidates, in addition to being well qualified to do the
work, possess intangible, harder-to-measure skills that would
prove to be a tremendous asset to a company. People with backgrounds in the humanities and other disciplines, for example,
might more successfully be able to apply some of the traits and
abilities listed in the *Future Work Skills 2020* report to business
problems. Potentially, they could do this in more creative and
innovative ways.

For instance, liberal arts graduates possess excellent criti-
cal- and abstract-thinking skills. Individuals schooled in the
humanities learn to weigh moral dilemmas and write clearly
on a broad range of knowledge spanning many areas. English
majors often make excellent project managers; they have faced
the challenge of reading *War and Peace*, then crafting a twenty-
five-page term paper on it, and completing the effort in five
days. These are people who are adept at schedules and deadlines.
But perhaps most importantly, people who study literature are
experienced in being transported into other cultures and diverse
environments through reading. They understand human nature

and can add enormous value toward making diversity and inclusion become realities in a company.

Ask yourself what your company or organization *really* needs. Question your assumptions and keep in mind that if your hiring patterns are skewed toward secular talent exclusively, your own actions could effectively and dramatically impede the diversity of thought and experience in your company. Consider how much your corporate progress could be enhanced by the collective differences of your employees. The key is in seeing diversity as a driver of innovation—and then working toward that reality.

Retaining and Engaging Employees

The number of women and minorities hired by an organization is irrelevant if these employees are not satisfied, valued employees, and are not retained by the organization. Most people want meaningful work that leverages their strengths and appeals to their aspirations. And they want to be fairly compensated and praised by their managers and peers, both privately and publicly.

Even if you've increased the diversity of your workforce in the number of hires, you still have the important task of creating and fostering a culture and environment that people want to be a part of. How do you build a successful, innovative organization that retains and fosters meaningful engagement with its employees, embracing all their differences?

Some companies, even highly successful ones, offer amazing enticements to create satisfaction among their employees. Free food, open workspaces, casual dress environments, on-site laundry services, and unlimited vacation time are touted as desirable, impressive offerings in many technology companies. But since a Google employee's average tenure is one year and one month, and

an Amazon employee's is one year,[11] clearly the perks alone are not keeping employees from leaving.

Companies that want to retain and engage their diverse and inclusive workforces are under pressure to offer not just perks but also something that recognizes the deep, intrinsic value of each of its employees.

WHAT WORKERS WANT AND NEED

People want meaningful lives, both at home and at work. Employees spend a lot of time at work. Companies must care about their workers and understand not only the reasons why employees leave but also why they stay. This requires that we make an effort to develop environments that support gender differences, cultural differences, and other key aspects of diversity.

Let's consider the concept of assimilation. When new people join an organization, assimilation is a standard goal; we need to make a new hire "one of us." This process, however, usually serves only to create a larger "in-group," and while well-intentioned, will likely derail corporate efforts to become inclusive, especially of employees who are women and/or underrepresented minorities.

Assimilation is an outdated concept that progressive organizations would do well to abandon, recognizing that it perpetuates an exclusionary environment. A person who cannot be assimilated into a group or company culture is considered not to be a "fit." Hiring employees who are just like us is familiar, natural, comfort-seeking behavior. We are mired in these ways due to psychological and brain-based influences. The reasons are understandable, and change is scary. Yet the results we want and need can only come when we intentionally draw upon the courage to hire differently. It is so much easier to stay within the comfort of our biases, but results cannot be obtained that way.

" *The results we want and need can only come when we intentionally draw upon the courage to hire differently.*"

VALUING WOMEN

Employees are far more likely to stay in an organization in which they have challenging, meaningful work; feel valued by leaders, managers, and peers for their contributions; and can be their authentic selves at work. It's important not to deal with people in just transactional ways. Being relational is often better and more needed. Females tend to be more relational than males,[12] hence another reason to have increasing numbers of them at various organizational levels. It behooves companies to create environments that embrace values of honesty, genuineness, and difference, and to actively work to eliminate behaviors that run counter to principles of psychological safety.

" *It's important not to deal with people in just transactional ways. Being relational is often better and more needed.*"

Perhaps it is not well understood that the handful of women who have succeeded in the current system are those who have widely adapted their style and approach to the patriarchal (male) model. They are valued less for their natural contributions and more for their male adaptations—in other words, they are valued for their sameness, not their difference! Leaning into a system of discrimination when we know that women are less likely than men to sit up front, interrupt, negotiate aggressively, and so on is tantamount to promoting sameness.

The acuteness of this mistake is significant when you consider that research across ninety-five different studies shows that while men have greater confidence in their leadership skills, women

have far greater competence.[13] Businesses benefit when women rise in an organization. If you're one of the people in charge (of a meeting, team, or company), however, you can tailor these behaviors, accounting for and working with these differences, thereby placing value on them.

> 66 *The handful of women who have succeeded in the current system are those who have widely adapted their style and approach to the patriarchal (male) model. They are valued less for their natural contributions and more for their male adaptations—in other words, they are valued for their sameness, not their difference!"*

We know that in meetings, women are more likely to be interrupted or ignored than men.[14] Knowing this, and wanting to mitigate this gender bias, the person in charge (or any group member wanting to support women at work) could intervene and say something like "Karla was just interrupted, and I'm curious to hear the rest of her thinking on this topic. Karla, please continue. Ron [the interrupter], you'll be next to speak."

Another approach could be to allow each person in the meeting an equal amount of time to share their ideas or make their pitch. Similarly, people from different cultures in which it's considered impolite to speak up can be encouraged to do so by an adept leader or group member who asks for their input. This person might say something like "Kumi, you've been quiet, but I'm aware that you're a subject matter expert. We're interested in hearing your thoughts on this topic."

Studies routinely show that advice given by men in the workplace is taken more seriously than advice given by women. Knowing this, what can we do? Leaders can communicate this

unfortunate reality to everyone who reports to them and publicly commit to changing this perception. Individuals can be taught to listen with intention when women speak and question any feelings about a woman's advice not being as valuable as that of a male peer.

When people surface their biases and lean into discomfort, those biases become malleable. Change is possible. But we have to work at it with intention and vigor, understanding that we all benefit when women are valued at work.

66 *When people surface their biases and lean into discomfort, those biases become malleable. Change is possible. But we have to work at it with intention and vigor, understanding that we all benefit when women are valued at work."*

Companies designing products and services used by women—who are fully half the global population and make 70% of purchasing decisions—stand to benefit hugely by having women design these products and figure out how best to market and sell them. Companies would also benefit by inviting more women to conceive of new products for them. Apple's health app, designed to track common and obscure things related to health, was not, when first launched, able to track menstrual cycles, an embarrassing oversight that need not have occurred if women were included in product design or review.

This work is about taking all that you know, continuing to learn about how women in the workplace are treated, and acting on that knowledge. It requires being observant of group communication and having a courage and willingness to intervene so that women are not held back, and everyone learns and grows.

VALUING OLDER AGE GROUPS

Millennials want to know there's purpose in what they do and to be able to develop skills that will take them to the next level. They also expect this in somewhat rapid timeframes. Although research shows that the greatest loyalty to an organization can be found among the Traditionalist (born between 1925 and 1945) and Boomer (1946–1964) generations, many companies today commonly over-focus on hiring millennials or younger workers. Maybe it's time for companies to begin a larger discussion about age bias or to run business case analyses to understand the cost of turnover in young hires measured against the retention of older, more experienced workers.

The world population is aging rapidly, making older workers a steady and reliable source of skilled workers with decades of experience. Hiring older workers can provide substantial benefits to business. In a diverse and inclusive company, older workers can often serve as mentors to younger employees. And since many older workers are not looking to advance their careers, they would have different motivations for helping others and thus prove well positioned to support and develop younger employees.

The cost of health coverage and a lack of technological prowess are often cited as reasons for not hiring older workers. Yet a recent *Tech Republic* report shows older workers to be just as, if not *more*, tech-savvy than younger workers.[15] Likewise, while health insurance rates do tend to increase with age, older workers frequently don't need the full range of health (family and maternity) benefits that younger workers require. And older workers, who understand the significant age bias they are up against, might tend to be highly appreciative of an employment offer and more loyal to a company. That loyalty is an offset to the costs associated with younger workers who change jobs with greater frequency.

Finally, an age-diverse workforce makes sense because older people make up the most substantial portion of the global marketplace. Older workers have purchasing power *and* are likely to have much higher insight into products that will appeal to them.

VALUING MINORITIES

Company leaders need to build and foster an environment of acceptance and inclusiveness in their workplaces. The biases people have about coworkers of different races can not only impede business growth and innovation but also lead to misunderstanding and discomfort that cause people to exit the organizations. Perspective is powerful. We would do well to create environments that deepen the empathy our employees have for one another. But how?

An Australian company called Diversifly (www.diversifly.com.au) offers virtual reality training programs designed to address unconscious bias in the workplace. Recognizing that people are experiential learners, its training programs develop scenarios in which people engage in experiences that allow them to feel compassion and empathy for others who are different from them. And the Virtual Human Interaction Lab at Stanford University has researchers designing scenarios to combat racial (and sexual) discrimination. Suppose a white man, for example, could enter a virtual room as a Black man (or woman) and experience what it *feels* like to be the minority in the room. Virtual reality gives credence to the old saying "Walk a mile in someone else's shoes if you really want to understand them." Imagine the possibilities for insightful learning that drives human behavior change and makes not only the workplace but also society better!

Companies have the opportunity *now* to leverage augmented reality as a learning tool to create psychological safety, helping people essentially get comfortable with their discomfort. How

better to relate to the point of view of another person than to step into that person's everyday life? Through virtual reality, we begin to practice a new kind of engagement with our diverse coworkers.

Performance Appraisals and "High-Potential" Employees

The author Anaïs Nin famously wrote, "We don't see things as they are, we see things as we are." She captured the powerful truth that the preconceived notions and biases that we (all people) have skew the way we see the world and the people in it. We're shaped by belief systems, family teachings, social norms, and life experiences. Just as these notions influence recruitment and hiring practices, they also affect the ways companies manage employee job performance.

This section will show you how current performance management systems hinder diversity and invite you to reengineer processes to support your D&I goals. I'll show you ways to alter employee evaluation methods to advance the diverse, inclusive, equitable workplace you desire.

Redefining Performance Management

Most mid- to large-size companies, and some smaller organizations, use an employee performance management process that typically works like this: once or twice a year, employees write a self-evaluation, highlighting their accomplishments to date, identifying areas for improvement, and giving themselves an overall rating. Employees submit their evaluations to their managers, who solicit input from other employees and then compute a final

grade, which is used to determine any compensation increase. This is shared with the employee at a later date.

This method of performance management is supposed to drive business results, reward employees for achievement, suggest areas of improvement, and help employees feel more engaged with the mission and business of their company. But recent analysis shows that just the opposite is true.[16] Here's what we know:

- Women tend to get promoted based on *performance,* while men get promoted based on *potential.*[17]

- Men are 30% more likely to be promoted to management and leadership roles than women.[18]

- Pay disparities exist and are significant between men, women, and underrepresented minorities doing the exact same work.[19]

Traditional performance management systems have really been about forced distribution rankings and quota systems. According to this, a certain amount of money is allocated for adjustments in salary, which are typically salary increases; employees are then graded, as you see in the image, in a bell curve of top, middle, and bottom performers. These systems falsely assume that men, women, and minorities are all promoted based on performance. Nowhere in the current evaluation processes do we account for the fact that while men have more confidence in their leadership skills, women have more competence; rather, white men continue to be promoted over women and minorities. The current systems perpetuate discrimination and hinder diversity, inclusion, engagement, and greater business success.

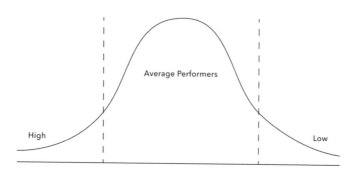

The stacked ranking approach, popularized among major corporations beginning in the 1980s with General Electric and others, uses a performance evaluation method that requires managers to assign a set percentage of employees to one of three-to-five categories. This means that a manager with a team of very high performers *must*, no matter what, designate a certain subset of employees to be low-performing, which is predicated on the assumption that a standard bell curve distribution is indicative of *all* groups. What happens with this approach is that employees and managers become pitted against one another; employees are often demoralized, especially if they plan to stay with the company, and feel as if they have no choice but to learn how the system works and to modify their behavior accordingly so that the system will work in their favor.

Grading on a curve is old-school, competitive, patriarchal thinking and is fundamentally bad for business. Instead of perpetuating this system, progressive managers and leaders would benefit by *reducing* the competition among their employees. They would need to change the traditional model, instead letting internal competition go for the sake of more innovation through

collaboration. They would need to act on removing pay disparities, promote more women and minorities into leadership roles,
and stop treating the differences between white men and others
as deficiencies but rather embrace those differences in the spirit
of a collaborative enterprise in which everyone benefits.

What would employees likely value more—competitive evaluation or ongoing coaching and development in an environment
designed around their perpetual success? The traditional annual
performance evaluation, with or without stacked ranking, is antiquated, outdated, and a time-consuming, expensive experience
that has little meaningful benefit. There was a time when the production of widgets on assembly lines, based solely on numeric
amounts, could leverage a ranking-style approach to improving
performance among workers; but that isn't relevant in today's
knowledge-based economy.

For us, work today largely involves collaborating with teams,
constantly enhancing our skills, and developing our abilities
over time. To be of real business value, performance management needs to focus more on continual human development and
less on competitive evaluation. Companies need to factor in the
knowledge that the ability to fairly evaluate performance can only
occur if false and harmful beliefs about genders, races, disabilities,
and other differences are not only discredited but also acted upon.

"High Potentials"

Employees should be expected to treat each other with respect,
but an insistence on prescribed sets of expected behaviors
does not take into consideration roles and scopes of work. The
so-called "high-potential" (hi-po) model in employee development is another example of forced distribution rankings. Typical

high-potential programs are akin to leadership development programs in that the elements of potential constitute a mix of 75% hard skills and 25% soft skills.

Assessments made of a given person's ability to transition quickly and successfully from individual contributor to manager, to director, to executive are next determined. (Titles vary in different companies, but the rise is from a lower level of contribution to a higher level of complexity with greater responsibility.) The assessments are largely subjective, involving a look at past performance evaluations (from HR), with input from line managers and others in the company with whom the person has interacted.

This approach assumes an iterative and linear nature to career development, which is frequently not the case in the modern business environment. Also, how does one interpret the value of employees not designated "high-potential"? Are they by default "low-potential" or "no-potential"?

Imagine an organizational system in which the performance of employees follows a "long-tail" curve (pictured) instead of a bell curve and in which a company is a community. Imagine in this system that individuals, dedicated to the success of their peers, are truly motivated by an inspiring vision of the future they help create. Business would resemble more of an ecosystem kept in balance by diversity of talent; it would gain strategic advantage by being flexible and better able to anticipate market shifts and adapt to, and even partner with, other businesses.

Technology companies often claim that they want to free their employees to be innovative and build a better world. But their organizational systems and processes speak more to exerting control over their female and minority employees based on their performance, while promoting white men based on their potential. This is not a welcoming environment for women or

underrepresented groups to want to be part of, much less to stay in for years.

Long-Tail Curve

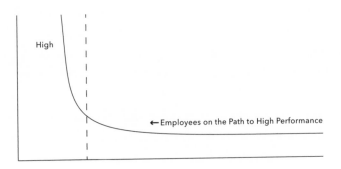

Women and minorities often benefit from having managers that coach them on political navigation and skills development. Yet managers are often criticized for not being good at or taking the time to provide coaching and regular feedback. In part, this is because feedback is a really great thing with a really bad rap. Feedback is information, feedback *always* tells something about the giver, and feedback is *always* controlled by the receiver. Since what I think about you says a lot about me, no feedback should be anonymous.

And yet, the feedback tool widely used in companies is called "360-degree feedback." It involves soliciting anonymous feedback from peers, managers, and others who have interacted with you. The idea is to provide a "safe" environment where others can honestly say how they perceive you. However, human behavior too often demonstrates that anonymity does not increase honesty but does increase mean-spirited behavior.

The Yik Yak app, launched in 2014, was developed by two young white males with the intention of allowing anonymity to advance democracy online, or at least within the two-mile radius

in which it works. There's no evidence to suggest a meaningful spread of democratic principles. However, Yik Yak has been used to bully transgender people, taunt suicidal individuals, harass college professors, and spew racial slurs. The anonymous sexual harassment of female video gamers is widespread, as are the number of trolls on Twitter that make rape, murder, and other horrendous threats. Anonymity undermines accountability.

Instead, to redesign an organizational system that will improve managerial coaching skills and enhance recipient value, I recommend developing a course around the concepts and principles in two excellent books, *What Did You Say? The Art of Giving and Receiving Feedback*[20] and *Triple Impact Coaching: Use-of-Self in the Coaching Process.*[21] In an often humorous way, *What Did You Say?* shows helpful processes for getting, giving, and analyzing feedback. It teaches us how to train ourselves not to take advice personally, but rather to consider it and think about the source that the guidance came from. This would allow the people receiving advice to learn and grow in both faster and more fulfilling ways. Imagine a healthy future workforce in which advice is provided and receivers anticipate it eagerly! This would be quite a dramatic change from the way feedback exchange works in most companies today. In a diverse and inclusive workforce, this kind of change builds trust and enables the advancement of women and underrepresented minorities in a company.

The other book, *Triple Impact Coaching*, is a complementary tome to *What Did You Say?* It communicates the value of self-knowledge as instrumental in understanding how you know, interact with, and coach others. The multilayered (triple) impact refers to a cascading coaching process that positively benefits layers of an organization. Senior leaders, middle managers, line employees, customers, and suppliers all benefit from

this interwoven approach. For companies building diversity and inclusion in their workforce, this type of coaching is a powerful enabler to help everyone thrive.

Inclusive Leadership

Humanists and *technology* are not words usually said in the same sentence. But to develop a diverse, multicultural workforce, it's necessary to develop and grow inclusive leaders. And inclusive leaders are humanists.[22] These leaders run effective companies not only by focusing on shareholder value but also by giving primary consideration to employee interests, values, and human dignity. Or, as Alan Loy McGinnis said, "There is no more noble occupation in the world than to assist another human being to help someone succeed."

It's often said that simple things are the most profound. One of the best definitions of effective leaders and managers I have heard is "Great leaders are those individuals who set out to make those around them better." Implicit in those words are essential qualities of inclusive leaders, people whom you trust to both work for the common good and share their success and who view their role as both a responsibility and a privilege. These men and women serve, listen, learn, engage, and optimize their own physical and emotional health to maintain their energy for caring for their employees.

66 *Inclusive leaders serve, listen, learn, engage, and optimize their own physical and emotional health to maintain their energy for caring for their employees."*

The Kaleel Jamison Consulting Group, Inc., of Troy, New York, lists twelve inclusive behaviors necessary to develop an environment

of "Conscious Inclusion: A work environment where we demonstrate and support behaviors that enable people—individually and collectively—to do their best work."[23] Do you and other leaders in your organization currently practice any of the following inclusive behaviors?

1. Greet people authentically—say hello.

2. Create a sense of "safety" for yourself and your team members.

3. Work for the common good and shared success.

4. Listen as an ally—listen, listen, listen, and then engage.

5. Lean into discomfort—be willing to challenge yourself and others.

6. Put your stake in the ground and be willing, eager, and able to move it.

7. Link to others' ideas, thoughts, and feelings.

8. Create shared vision—ask others to share their thoughts and experiences, accepting their frame of reference as true for them.

9. Address misunderstandings and resolve disagreements.

10. Speak up when people are being excluded.

11. Ask who else needs to be in the room to understand the whole situation.

12. Build trust—do what you say you will do and honor confidentiality.

Most employees do what managers and leaders expect them to do, which makes their clearly articulated expectations critical to success. This presents a special challenge to those organizations with low or flat structures in which informal communication is often the norm. It's especially difficult for technology companies, especially start-ups in which policies that support diversity of talent have not been clearly defined and communicated, to develop a varied workforce.

The well-documented and often-replicated Milgram experiment of the 1950s demonstrated that people will do cruel things, especially if they can be anonymous, when an authority figure gives the go-ahead.[24] Yale University psychologist Stanley Milgram set up the experiment to measure the willingness of participants to obey authority. Participants were to deliver increasingly higher levels of electric shocks (up to 450 volts) to people they did not know well and could not see. The person delivering the shock was called the teacher, and the person receiving the shock was called the learner. Teachers asked learners to match word pairs, and when learners failed, teachers were told by a separate authority to deliver shocks—in increasingly high voltages for each error committed. In reality, no shocks were delivered, though learners played their role by sometimes screaming in pain or asking for the experiment to stop.

This experiment showed how much pain an average person would be willing to inflict on another if they were ordered to do so, even when the infliction of pain was counter to their beliefs about the humane treatment of others. This experiment indicates to us that relatively few people have the ability to resist direct authority.

But consider the following positive learning from the experiment: because employees do tend to obey authority, companies must clearly articulate, document, and enforce expectations about

appropriate behavior toward others. It's not okay to be biased just because everyone has unconscious biases. Surfacing your biases and then taking action to mitigate them needs to be valued and encouraged. Treating coworkers with respect needs to be expected at all times. Sexism is not acceptable; and the harassment of female employees is not only against the law but also must become a zero-tolerance policy in every firm. People largely do what leaders expect them to do, so be extremely precise and maintain accountability for what to expect and what to tolerate in the way people treat each other throughout your organization.

    “ *People largely do what leaders expect them to do,*
      so be extremely precise and maintain accountability
      for what to expect and what to tolerate in the way
      people treat each other throughout your organization.”

A company that wants to be representative of diverse talent will not succeed if employees have to make compromises that run counter to their values. Collaboration beyond mere tolerance of difference is necessary for inclusivity. Leaders and managers must learn the art of humble inquiry and encourage a climate of speaking up.

    “ *Collaboration beyond mere tolerance of*
      difference is necessary for inclusivity.”

Research suggests that there are two types of factors that affect whether or not people speak up at work. The first is individual differences and includes inborn personality traits (for example, introversion versus extroversion), communication skills, and personal concerns about job security. The second is context

and refers to organizational factors that provide cues about how speaking up is received, such as leader behavior, work group, and organizational structure.[25]

Leaders proficient in the art of humble inquiry show genuine interest in others as individuals. They ask questions, listen carefully, and ask more questions, always seeking to understand. These leaders challenge their natural tendency to make assumptions about others based on culture, background, or other factors. Through these behaviors, they genuinely appreciate the uniqueness of others and learn from them.

> " *Leaders proficient in the art of humble inquiry show genuine interest in others as individuals. They ask questions, listen carefully, and ask more questions, always seeking to understand.*"

Fitting In

Lakeisha, a sixteen-year veteran of an established $50-billion insurance company, approached me while we were walking out to the shared parking garage after work. She enthusiastically shared with me that for the first time in all the years she'd worked here, an executive approached her at a company event, introduced himself, and asked questions about her. He was kind, humble, and inquisitive, and she expressed that she felt genuinely listened to for the first time in her tenure.

This surprised me, and I asked what typically happens when she meets an executive. Sixteen years at a company is a long time not to feel like someone wants to listen to you. She replied that she is generally overlooked because she is

Continued

"just" an assistant to a middle manager. Lakeisha then told me she worried the executive would either not last long at the company because his willingness and ability to be authentic would cause the other senior leaders to look bad, or else he would eventually be pressured into modifying his behavior to fit in and become "one of them."

To what degree does your company culture require employees to compromise their authenticity and values? Do you feel that you have to hide parts of your identity when you go to work? Could this be why many women and minority hires in companies don't stay? And do you rationalize their departures with the excuse "They're just not a fit here"?

Norms set by the founders and leaders of a company govern its culture. It's important that leaders learn and model both a cultural and personal humility (about what they can accomplish on their own) in order to be able to succeed at meeting the corporate D&I challenge. A common saying among organizational development experts, that "Culture eats strategy for lunch," captures an important truth for us. As you think about how to become the kind of inclusive leader who effects positive change in your company's workplace culture, remember that culture *always* trumps strategy. And effective strategy implementation requires a supportive culture.

Do you believe you are an inclusive and culturally responsive leader? Ask yourself the following questions:

1. Do you correct biased decision-making by becoming actively aware of your unconscious biases and move forward with the serious intention to overcome those implicit associations that drive your behavior?

2. Do you consider racial, ethnic, age, gender, disability, personality, and other differences when you make work assignments so you can help promote the interplay of cultural and work style differences? Do you encourage the development of diverse, inclusive, high-performing teams?

3. Do you champion diversity of thought by actively listening to all employees—especially those whose opinions and ideas are different from your own— seeking to understand and making sure there is full, clear communication?

4. Do you create a work environment that values dignity, respect, and differences among employees?

5. Do you recognize, publicly acknowledge, and actively work to communicate that "fit" is both a myth and an excuse used to maintain exclusivity and homogeneity?

6. Do you measure the cultural competence of your workforce and share that information transparently with the workforce?

If yes, congratulations! If no, when will you begin?

Quick Summary

Here are some key points to remember from this chapter:

- Finding and hiring for diversity requires new, creative, nontraditional approaches.

- There is no pipeline problem. Plenty of women and underrepresented minorities exist with the talent that businesses need.

- Most of the students attending elite schools come from wealthy families with lots of connections, and selections exclusive to this pool generally represent hiring for sameness, not difference. Recruit creatively and also from elsewhere.

- Interviewer bias is real, and it can be prevented. Lean into discomfort with applicants who are not like you. Remember that this feeling is often about you, not them. And interview applicants with the intention of discovering valuable differences. Practice holistic hiring.

- "Culture fit" and "lowering the bar" are myths that reinforce discrimination in our companies.

- Inclusion must be a core value, embedded in the organization, for changes in recruitment, hiring, and engagement to work.

- Virtual reality is a powerful tool we can use to "walk in someone else's shoes" and develop empathy. Engaging minorities and those who are different from us in the workplace allows us to retain them, which leads to greater innovation and a better way of doing business.

- Embrace humility and develop curiosity about difference.

- Don't limit yourself to just buying talent. Build talent, and develop people.

Action Steps

Need to know how to apply what you just read? Here are some steps and ideas:

- Communicate that lack of pipeline is not a problem, but the current *thinking* about pipeline is an issue that you are committed to overcome.
  - State clear, concrete expectations for how your organization will more forward to redesign existing and historical processes used by the HR department.

- Redesign and reengineer the recruitment, hiring, engagement, and performance management systems and processes that are in place today to remove the unintentional discrimination built into them.

- Leverage virtual and augmented reality as a transformative teaching tool to understand and embrace the experiences of women and underrepresented minorities in the workforce.

- Abandon "not a fit" as a reason for not hiring (or for firing). Demand clear, substantiated, verifiable reasons.

- Learn and apply the key behaviors of inclusive leaders.

Learning to Navigate Difference

We're all interconnected and that's a really beautiful thing.
We have links to everyone else in our lives and in the world. . . .
You can celebrate that there are connections everywhere.

—JANE SEYMOUR

Diversity is, in truth, an acquired taste. When we have not had any substantive and meaningful exposure to people who are not like us, it's difficult to develop an appreciation for them. Our enjoyment of others comes as we begin the process of knowing them and valuing the differences and similarities we share. When the topic of diversity arises at work, people often evidence either an attitude of indifference or a sense of anxiety about managing conflict. You'll often hear statements like:

"That's really not a problem here."

"We have lots of diversity in our workforce."

"We have diversity initiatives in place here; we're managing the issue."

"The company produces great results and is highly profitable. Why change?"

"Our work assignments and hiring decisions are based on merit, competency, and skill."

"With all these different views, it's going to take forever to find common ground. Why can't we all just agree?"

"We can't discuss gender or racial equity—it's just too emotionally charged. It doesn't belong at work."

"Oh, no—are we going to be facing a discrimination lawsuit?"

Meaningful conversations about diversity are not for the faint of heart. Talking about race, gender, sexual orientation, religion, and other human differences and perspectives in a work group can cause discomfort. As someone looking to bring about change in an organization, you'll need to expect and manage the possible outcomes these meaningful conversations can bring. Lack of trust, concern about disrespect, and the potential for interpersonal conflict are very real scenarios you'll need to calmly and respectfully navigate. However, done well, the opportunity to interact with mixed-perspective groups also gives everyone in your workforce the chance to consider alternate views, experiences, and thoughts.

In this chapter, I'll show you how to begin having important conversations about diversity with people in your organization. You'll learn ways to assess your company's readiness, prepare for different communication styles, understand the dimensions of diversity and inclusion, and facilitate the conversations. These are not easy conversations to have; and in a group setting, the time it takes to be able to reach consensus—when that is the goal—will likely be longer than for conversations that are less emotionally charged.

But the process of getting there will be done with a heightened anticipation of discovery and positive outcomes. Consensus aside, the time it takes for each person to feel that they have been truly listened to and honestly heard is invaluable to creating the kind of inclusivity and understanding of difference that spurs

amazing performance. We'll talk about all this in light of the bigger picture, recognizing that it's not just workforce diversity we're aiming for but vibrant, authentic, dynamic workplace inclusion.

Dimensions of Diversity and Inclusion

Bernardo Ferdman, editor of *Diversity at Work: The Practice of Inclusion*, defines diversity as "the representation of multiple identity groups and their cultures in a particular organization or work group."[1] He also suggests that diversity alone does not confer benefits but rather requires that additional conditions in an organization or group be present. One of these conditions is inclusion, which according to Ferdman "involves how well organizations and their members fully connect with, engage, and utilize people across all types of differences."[2]

I share this with you because I've come to see that conversations that truly shift thinking and perspective come from not just diverse but also inclusive workplaces where self-reflection and open communication are valued. We need diversity and honest, open conversation, but our workplaces will not truly transform until we build, foster, and sustain an environment of inclusivity. Only then will our organizations be able to achieve and function at their full potential. And only then will we be able to innovate and succeed in a way that impacts the industries we're part of and society as a whole.

> *Inclusion is about what it feels like to be an individual, team, leader, supplier, or customer, since at its essence, it's about valuing people because of their differences (and similarities) to us."*

The simple reality of an inclusive workplace lies in how leaders, managers, employees, vendors, and customers experience it. This is about what it *feels* like to be an individual, team, leader, supplier, or customer, since inclusion, at its essence, is about valuing people because of their differences (and similarities) to us. Conversations that shift thinking bring those differences into positive perspective.

What kinds of differences in people might we encounter that will strengthen us and enlarge our understanding of the world? We'll come across both visible and invisible differences in our workforces, as well as people who claim and reject aspects of their identities in varying situations. We need to intentionally and proactively be willing to take steps to begin enacting change, treading carefully but moving forward. And as we do this, we'll want to keep in mind the many layers and facets of identities, or what we experience as dimensions of diversity and inclusion that we may find in these daily interactions. This includes:

- Personality—different styles and characteristics
- Internal dimensions—age, gender, sexual orientation, mental ability, physical ability, ancestry, and race
- External dimensions—geographic location, income, personal habits, recreational habits, religion, educational background, work experience, appearance, parental status, and marital status
- Organizational dimensions—functional level/classification, work content/field, division/department, business unit, work group, seniority, work location, union affiliation, and management status

Each of these dimensions lies on a spectrum where it makes a little difference, a great difference, or something in between in

how people are treated in your organization. To prepare your-self for learning to navigate differences, reflect on which of these dimensions seem to most impact and influence how people are treated. Think about how these differences in treatment are demonstrated and what this says about your company values relative to diversity and inclusion.

Conversations That Shift Thinking

Most people have topics they discuss at work and other topics they discuss outside work, with clear boundaries between the two. We generally know that not all conversations make sense in workplace settings. But what happens when we avoid important topics, topics that affect us, topics that truly need to be talked about?

With issues of diversity and inclusion, progressive companies are increasingly coming to understand that it's both difficult and foolhardy to formally separate social good from organizational purpose. They're finding that they need to listen to and learn from their employees in a different way and that not doing so impacts the way they do business.

> 66 *Progressive companies are increasingly coming to understand that it's both difficult and foolhardy to formally separate social good from organizational purpose.*"

We need to begin having conversations that shift and elevate our thinking, our interactions, and our work. This requires a paradigm shift in our companies but also a change in our personal approach. The advice, research, and action items I've provided in this book offer you a guiding framework for doing this important work;

but it will take your courage, perseverance, creativity, and fortitude to carry it out so that you see the results. Imagine a vibrant, productive, innovative workforce that reflects the true diversity of our human experience. Imagine an inclusive organization that brings out the best in *all* its people, operating at its highest potential.

Talking about Things That Matter

In order for us to successfully navigate our differences, we need to be able to talk about things that matter. This means that we have respectful, intentional conversations to learn about our colleagues and share about ourselves. This means that we hold out-of-the norm conversations, which may be uncomfortable at first. This means that we begin a dialogue to not only show our genuine interest in others but also communicate that we care about workforce diversity and inclusion as a whole. When we do this enough, we engage others and normalize conversations about things that matter. Our out-of-the-norm conversations begin to hold a different promise.

From 2014 to the present time, videotaped killings of unarmed Black men by police have increasingly and disturbingly made national headline news. Issues of racism and sexism on university campuses have also appeared with regularity in the media. People are talking about immigration, discrimination, harassment, and prejudice more and more outside work settings.

But don't these realities touch and affect every one of us or at least someone we know? Don't we carry our thoughts and feelings about these around with us, and don't they, at least in some part, inform our interactions with coworkers who are different from us? Dr. Arin Reeves, author of "Some Uncomfortable Truths," appropriately asks, "How can we possibly be expected

to deal with differences adequately in the workplace when we cannot even really talk about the ways in which differences are influencing the most intense of current events around us?"[3]

BREAKING THROUGH SILENCE

So I ask: Is silence inadvertently used in your organization to serve the purpose of maintaining relationships and social order?

Race, sex, politics, and religion are topics that most of us have been socialized not to discuss at work. And the sexual or religious preferences of colleagues is not information that lends itself to workplace sharing anyway.

But if the national news presents the story of the horrific murder of a young gay man, is it not sometimes reasonable to check in on the feelings of employees, especially those who are openly gay? Likewise, when defenseless Black men are killed over minor traffic violations, should managers and leaders not check in on the feelings and well-being of Black employees with whom they have established respectful, caring relationships?

But how do you do this in your own organization? How do you know what to say? Even worse, what if you say the wrong thing? Not all managers or leaders are equipped to do this well, so our defense is to escape into silence. Yet the employees hardest hit by that silence may be in the minority groups that are afraid to share their feelings without being ostracized or worrying their careers could be compromised.

We need to equip ourselves with skills that will enable us to respectfully navigate through the silence and status quo in our workplaces and begin talking about things that matter. Speaking up for what's right isn't easy. It requires learning a new way to communicate amid fear, uncertainty, and the unknown. And it is a process that takes practice and unfolds over time.

" *We need to equip ourselves with skills that*
will enable us to respectfully navigate through
the silence and status quo in our workplaces
and begin talking about things that matter."

Effective leaders begin this work by focusing first on groups. Merck Pharmaceutical's CEO Kenneth Frazier offered a powerful public statement in the aftermath of a white-supremacy rally where a counterprotester was killed. Speaking about the response from senior government officials, Frazier said: "America's leaders must honor our fundamental values by clearly rejecting expressions of hatred, bigotry, and group supremacy, which run counter to the American ideal that all people are created equal."[4]

Other CEOs across the United States immediately expressed their agreement with and support of Frazier's statement. Ken Frazier's action is a good example of the courageous leadership required when business leaders wade into important issues of social justice.

Bernard Tyson, CEO of Kaiser Permanente, a $62-billion healthcare organization, wrote a powerful public essay in 2014 titled "It's Time to Revolutionize Race Relations." This came in response to a growing number of killings of unarmed Black men across the United States. He also issued an internal memo to company employees saying, in part: "Throughout our history, we have consistently taken a stand for equality—and *against* discrimination. . . . We are firm in our belief . . . that our differences have the capacity to make us stronger. . . . As heartbreaking as recent events have been, I take heart in the overwhelming goodness, decency, and justice shown by Americans all over our great country. That gives me hope. . . . We will not tolerate racism or discrimination of any kind. We will continue to champion diversity, inclusion, and equity to achieve equality for *all*."[5]

These two examples demonstrate leadership courage and effectiveness to publicly and internally address social justice issues. But the challenge goes beyond bold public statements. When addressing employees in your company, work group, or team, consider following these guidelines:

- Share your feelings and your intention—"I am distraught at the recent news about the prevailing issues of racism in our communities. I want to have a constructive and respectful conversation about this topic."

- Share why you think it's important to discuss this—"I'm bringing this up because I value all of you as colleagues and I don't want anyone to interpret silence as not caring. This is an important issue."

- Seek to understand and listen attentively with a willingness to learn—"I want to understand your perspectives."

- Make clarifying statements to promote group dialogue—"I'm not sure I follow you. Please say more."

At the end of these conversations, wrap up the dialogue and say "thank you" to everyone present. By behaving in an authentic, genuine manner, you will be communicating to employees that you care not just about the issue of racism but about *them*.

66 *When you are authentic and genuine, you communicate to employees that you care not just about the issue of racism but about* them.*"*

Mandela Schumacher-Hodge, in a piece titled "My White Boss Talked About Race in America and This Is What Happened,"[6] shares her story of profound gratitude for Freada Kapor Klein, her

boss who communicated the message "I care about you as a colleague and a person. I knew you'd be troubled by the police murders of Black men, as everyone should be, so I wanted to open the space for you to talk about it with me, if you chose to do so."[7] This gesture of compassion allowed Schumacher-Hodge the opportunity to share the trauma she felt in a psychologically safe space.

Dr. Kapor Klein is a stellar role model for other leaders to learn from. She could have elected to stay in the safety of not discussing these tragic events, but she chose instead to reach out to the people who work for her with compassion and genuine concern. The positive results from her action include having employees who know with certainty that they matter as people, not just as workers, which builds trust and loyalty both to the company and to its leader.

As the sense of psychological safety grows in your company's culture, people will feel greater engagement and be more ready to discuss relevant, challenging topics, like the gender pay gap, racial inequities in the workplace, or other important situations covered in the news. We do well when we tackle these subjects in a way that complements our company's mission and clarifies its vision for the future.

> 66 *As the sense of psychological safety grows in your company's culture, people will feel greater engagement and be more ready to discuss relevant, challenging topics."*

Assessing Your Company's Readiness

In recent years, hundreds of organizations have professed the importance and value of diverse workforces, publicly stating their

commitment to bring about change.[8] But there have been few results to show for it. How do you gauge your company's readiness to tackle the important conversations? Even if leaders in your organization have the best of intentions and a genuine willingness to change the way things work, how do you avoid getting in over your head?

In her book *We Can't Talk about That at Work!*, Mary-Frances Winters shares some excellent questions company leaders can use to assess organizational readiness.[9] For example:

- Is inclusion clearly articulated as one of the organization's values?

- Does the organization demonstrate that it values inclusion through leader actions?

- Is diversity of the workforce visible at all organizational levels?

- Are leaders and managers adept at supporting women and minority employee development?

- What is the level of trust in leadership and management?

Conversations that shift thinking work best when people first manage their individual implicit associations, as this helps prepare them for the reflection that meaningful dialogue requires. And it is imperative that leaders reject unsavory behavioral norms as group values in their organizations. To accomplish any of this, you must prepare in advance.

Tools to Prepare for Navigating Differences

We can engage with people in our companies in meaningful, responsive, and eye-opening ways. Some of the tools at our disposal

allow us to collect data and learn more about how our employees feel and what they really think. Other tools require us to introduce new practices and ideas to our companies, interrupting the status quo. Different tools work better in some situations than others, and their effectiveness will often depend on how we introduce them, model them, and uphold them in our companies. To successfully cultivate an inclusive workplace where we navigate well, embracing our differences means that we are creative, in tune with the existing culture of our companies, and courageous about trying new things. In this section, I'll provide you with some ideas to get you started.

EMPLOYEE SURVEYS

The qualities most of us desire in coworkers revolve around acceptance. We look for characteristics such as kindness, honesty, trust, and patience in one another. Navigating differences in the workplace also means cultivating inclusive qualities, which requires that we refrain from judgment and criticism and choose connection and inquiry to satisfy our curiosities. This requires a major shift in mindset, maturity, and the development and use of our critical-thinking skills.

One way we can determine our organizational standing in this realm is to measure the inclusiveness of our current workforces and then act upon the feedback we receive. You could, for example, ask employees to respond to statements and questions like:

1. I feel valued as an individual at [company name].
   a. strongly agree
   b. agree
   c. neutral
   d. disagree
   e. strongly disagree

2. The people I work with treat each other with respect, valuing gender, race, age, ethnicity, religion, sexual orientation, disability, or any other difference.
   a. strongly agree
   b. agree
   c. neutral
   d. disagree
   e. strongly disagree

3. In my department, division, business unit, or work team, I feel comfortable voicing my opinions and ideas, even when they are different from those of others.
   a. strongly agree
   b. agree
   c. neutral
   d. disagree
   e. strongly disagree

4. In what ways could the company environment be changed to help you feel more included?

   _____

   _____

5. What actions could the company take to become more appealing in order to retain female employees?

   _____

   _____

6. What actions could the company take to become more appealing in order to retain underrepresented minority employees?

   _____

   _____

7. I work in an intentionally diverse and inclusive environment.
   a. strongly agree
   b. agree
   c. neutral
   d. disagree
   e. strongly disagree

After gathering the survey data, you can segment it by a variety of differences, such as answers given by men versus those given by women, and answers produced by people of different races, ethnicities, and age groupings. Analyses like these provide insights into how various populations within an organization experience the company and offer ideas for actions that you can take to improve the environment for everyone.

This survey information also establishes a baseline set of inclusion metrics to help leaders guide future organizational endeavors. Let employees know that this survey and the follow-up actions to it are examples of the organization's commitment to diversity and inclusion. It is imperative that company leaders act on the feedback received from the survey. This critical action establishes and helps maintain leadership credibility concerning D&I.

Let some time pass after you've surveyed the employees and taken steps based on their feedback. Then survey again six to twelve months later and compare your new results to the baseline you established with the original survey. With each improvement, your employees and company become more inclusive, and hence better at navigating the differences among themselves.

PERSONALITY AND STRENGTHS TESTS

Another way companies can learn to navigate differences and cultivate inclusion in their workplaces is to take a look at the strengths, work preferences, and personalities of their employees. Companies commonly use different tools to develop insights about their employees. The Myers-Briggs Type Indicator, or MBTI, are interesting assessments that reveal personality preferences and types, and StrengthsFinder, DiSC, and Enneagram measure for areas of particular strengths in individuals.

Measures of emotional intelligence, or EQ, are of particular value when working to develop diverse and inclusive workplaces, as these tests provide information about a person's ability to recognize, evaluate, and regulate their emotions, as well as perceive and interpret the feelings of other individuals and groups of people. And EQ is correlated with job success, whereas IQ is not.

In addition to helping our individual employees learn about themselves, we can leverage information from these tools to help build teams that assure input from those with different strengths, viewpoints, and talents.

Similarly, if organizations selected categories such as race, age, and gender on the Implicit Association Test (IAT) and examined the output, that data could also help ensure diversity of bias on teams. When we have more information about our employees and teams and know how they work best, we can better navigate differences and create an environment that is productive and satisfying for our employees, leading to greater respect, retention, engagement, and performance.

CULTURAL COMPETENCE INVENTORIES

Cultural competence is our ability to understand, appreciate, and interact with people who come from cultures or belief systems

different from our own. I highly recommend to organizational leaders that they measure the cultural competence of their existing workforces. This allows them to determine if their employees are ready to support and truly commit to diversity and inclusion. Corporate leaders will need to act swiftly and imaginatively on the information they receive. There are a number of tools available for this purpose, which can be leveraged at individual, group, and organization-wide levels.

One such tool is the Intercultural Development Inventory (IDI™), a validated psychometric instrument that's been available since 1997 and has been used by more than 500,000 people worldwide. The IDI measures cultural competence for individuals and groups based on a six-stage sequence: denial, defense, minimization, acceptance, adaptation, and integration. IDI findings have shown that just as managers often perceive themselves as being better leaders than they actually are (based on measurement tools and feedback from their direct reports), so too do we overestimate our diversity skills. A full 90% of people measured said they believe they have a well-developed multicultural level of competence, while in reality only 13% actually do.[10]

We tend to minimize the importance of diversity and inclusion because we operate on the false assumption that others share the same core values and beliefs we do. The more we can develop ourselves as "cultural detectives," people with innate curiosity about others who are *not* like us, the greater value we will collectively generate—and this supports how we learn to navigate the differences among us. Consider measuring for the cultural competence of your employee base. It's an essential tool that will allow you to build greater inclusivity in your workforce.

COMMUNICATION STYLE INVENTORIES

Businesses are often composed of people from differing nationalities. I believe gaining a broad understanding of the differences among cultures is a necessary first step in identifying communication styles that can aid us in navigating differences. One useful tool, the International Conflict Style Inventory, is a cross-culturally valid assessment tool for identifying effective approaches for dialogue across cultural differences.[11]

According to this inventory, the four preferred styles include:

- **Discussion style**—Typically direct and more emotionally controlled, this style is favored by Euro-American, Northern European, and Canadian cultures.

- **Engagement style**—Also direct but emotionally more expressive, this style is typically preferred by African-Americans, Greeks, some Western Europeans, and many South American and Latino cultures.

- **Accommodation style**—Often the preferred choice of most Asian cultures, this style is indirect and emotionally reserved.

- **Dynamic style**—Common among Middle Eastern cultures, this style is characterized as indirect and emotionally expressive.

Communication styles in these four different categories indicate what people in a given culture often think of as natural, healthy, and correct. The categories also provide an excellent indication of how people from certain cultures may judge the behaviors of others. Most of us assume that others think as we do, and within cultures, there is some truth to that. But between

differing cultures, we need to understand those assumptions first before engaging in uncommon workplace conversations.

Keep in mind that these communication styles *generally* depict varying cultures. Individuals are unique, and styles may overlap or exist in differing degrees based on the environment someone was raised in. But being aware of these communication styles can also help us navigate workplace differences as a whole, allowing us to be sensitive to coworkers and providing us with insight about how we might personally come across to others.

Determining Your Own Self-Readiness

Learning to navigate differences among people is a significant undertaking in any organization. Leaders, managers—indeed, most of us—are not accustomed to having a bold dialogue about social issues that affect people at work. Just as we need to know ourselves to manage our unconscious biases, we also need to determine our readiness to handle potential conflicts that may arise from sensitive discussions. We would not climb a mountain or run a marathon without deciding our readiness and working to become as prepared as possible. It's just as important to assess our self-readiness to navigate differences.

Determining Your Conflict-Management Styles

Once we've determined our organizational readiness, it's imperative that we find out the conflict-management preferences and abilities of our discussion leaders. Talking about race, gender, politics, and other often-polarizing topics easily leads to conflicting feelings and uncomfortable, sometimes unpleasant dialogue. Whoever is

driving the debate must first gain insight into their own skill level in managing potential conflict.

The Thomas-Kilmann Conflict Mode Instrument (TKI),[12] used more than eight million times over four decades, is an excellent tool we can use to develop or increase our own self-awareness. The TKI is designed to give us insight into a person's preferred behavior in conflict situations. When there's conflict, we've learned that people typically behave either assertively or cooperatively, depending on the desire and ability they have to satisfy their concerns, the concerns of others, or both.

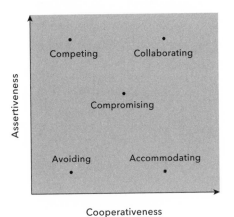

Within the behavioral dimensions of assertion and cooperation are five different modes we can use for responding to conflict. From the TKI:

- **Competing** is assertive and uncooperative, a power-oriented mode. When competing, an individual pursues his or her own concerns at the other person's expense, using whatever power seems appropriate to win his or her position.

Competing might mean standing up for your rights, defending a position you believe is correct, or simply trying to win.

- **Collaborating** is both assertive and cooperative. When collaborating, an individual attempts to work with the other person to find a solution that fully satisfies the concerns of both. It involves digging into an issue to identify the underlying concerns of the two individuals and to find an alternative that meets both sets of concerns. Collaborating between two persons might take the form of exploring a disagreement to learn from each other's insights, resolving some condition that would otherwise have them competing for resources, or confronting and trying to find a creative solution to an interpersonal problem.

- **Compromising** is intermediate in both assertiveness and cooperativeness. When compromising, the objective is to find an expedient, mutually acceptable solution that partially satisfies both parties. Compromising falls on a middle ground between competing and accommodating, giving up more than competing but less than accommodating. Likewise, it addresses an issue more directly than avoiding but doesn't explore it in as much depth as collaborating. Compromising might mean splitting the difference, exchanging concessions, or seeking a quick middle-ground position.

- **Accommodating** is unassertive and cooperative—the opposite of competing. When accommodating, an individual neglects his or her own concerns to satisfy the concerns of the other person; there is an element of self-sacrifice in this mode. Accommodating might take the form of selfless generosity or charity, obeying another

person's order when you would prefer not to, or yielding to another's point of view.

- **Avoiding** is unassertive and uncooperative. When avoiding, an individual does not immediately pursue his or her own concerns or those of the other person. He or she does not address the conflict. Avoiding might take the form of diplomatically sidestepping an issue, postponing an issue until a better time, or simply withdrawing from a threatening situation.[13]

All people use all five conflict-handling modes at varying times. No one has a single style of dealing with conflict. But most of us are more comfortable with some modes than others, and so we rely on those modes more often. How you manage conflict stemming from a discussion of sensitive topics in the workplace is a result of your own personal predispositions and the requirements of a given situation. The TKI is designed to measure this mix of conflict-handling modes and provide you with insight to help you manage the out-of-the-norm conversations that increasingly need to happen in the workplace.

Writing a Brief Biography

Another useful way to embark on the journey of determining self-readiness for navigating differences is to write your own brief three- to five-page biography. This doesn't require that you produce a masterpiece, only that you are honest with yourself. A biography of this sort will enable you to notice and reflect upon your experiences and underlying belief systems. You can use it as a tool to explore and think further about the influences

in your life—specifically your values and beliefs about yourself and others.

After you finish it, consider sharing your bio with a trusted colleague to encourage deep listening and questioning, allowing you to further explore cultural curiosity. If you can get others in your company to write and share their own biographies, think of the way this could create connection, build empathy, and enhance meaning in the work environment.

Here are some questions you can answer in your brief biography:

- As a child, what were you taught to believe about how to treat others?
- What kinds of activities and behaviors were you praised for while growing up?
- What kinds of activities and behaviors were frowned upon?
- What were you taught to believe about time, family, money, and work?
- What were you taught about people who did not share your family's beliefs?
- How connected were you to your community (school, town, place of religious worship, cultural groups)?
- Did your family discuss race or racial differences?
- As a child, what were your dreams for the future?
- How has race, class, or gender influenced your life, in terms of what you believe you could accomplish?
- Describe how easy or difficult it has been for you to attain each of the following:

- Education
- Medical care
- Work
- Food
- Housing
- Transportation
- Legal protection
- A support network
- A sense of belonging
- Do you identify primarily as someone who is lucky, privileged, or blessed? Why?

Be creative about tools you use in your companies. You can do more than collect information or invite employees to reflect on their individual, unconscious biases and beliefs. The following section will help you explore some specific ways to normalize and mainstream cultural curiosity, building them into the fiber of your organizations.

Preparing to Manage Group Process

After establishing both your organization's fitness and your self-readiness, you'll want to prepare for managing the group's process. This means you'll establish tenets for how people will treat one another as they're having the conversations that help shift thinking. This also lays an important foundation that needs to become standard practice in this type of organizational development work.

Here are some suggested rules of engagement for anyone participating in a sensitive conversation. These need to be shared, revised, and agreed upon by everyone before any discussion begins.

- **Talk**—Reflect, first considering your conscious and unconscious biases. Then be active and participate.

- **Speak one person at a time**—Do not have sidebar conversations or interrupt when people are talking.

- **Be succinct**—Do not dominate the conversation.

- **Listen**—Go for understanding, not winning by making a point at the cost of others.

- **Stay fully present**—Pay attention to others, refraining from the use of phones and devices or allowing for other distractions.

- **Accept the views of others**—Challenge others with respect, criticizing the idea if you need to, but not the person.

- **Abandon assumptions**—Don't assume that knowing what's good for you means knowing what's good for others. Aim for mutual understanding instead.

- **No retribution**—Don't criticize people after the meeting for their honesty and openness during the meeting, even if you didn't agree.

- **Confidentiality**—Use your best judgment about what, if anything, you want to share and with whom.

- **Start and stop on time**—Take responsible actions that show respect for the leader, facilitator, and participants and the time they're giving to have the conversations that matter.

Once the group has reached consensus on the rules of engagement, the facilitator must let everyone know that each person is free to speak up if they see a violation of the rules, and that the discussion leader will do the same. Should this occur, the conversation will pause for reflection before proceeding. If

repeated offenses occur, the offender may be asked to leave the physical space.

Facilitating Conversations

After setting expectations and ensuring that everyone has a clear understanding of the ground rules for group conversations, you're ready to begin talking. Think about your goals, remember the big picture, and consider the people who will be involved in the conversation. You'll want to make the environment conducive to a good discussion, prepare your thoughts, and also ready yourself for the unexpected. As I mentioned before, having these conversations takes courage and requires your willingness to accept some discomfort.

Here are some helpful questions and topics for your group to consider as you begin talking:

- How does your company or team decide which problems are worth solving? How many of these problems involve inclusion, diversity, innovation, or belonging?

- How do different identities—for example, cultural identity, job (role) identity, and gender identity—intersect?

- Many assumptions and beliefs are commonly held about whites, Blacks, Asians, Hispanics, men, children, women, and seniors. Let's talk about stereotypes versus archetypes and how we use each. (Stereotypes are widely held, fixed, and oversimplified ideas of types of people, which are often racist, sexist, homophobic, or disparaging in other ways. Archetypes are typical examples or models of certain people or things and are not derogatory or laden with negative value.)

Remember that you will feel tension and unease while engaging in these challenging discussions, and that's okay. Facilitate the discussions with great care, listen well, question your assumptions, and learn. You are doing something so right. Cultural preferences, individual biographies, inborn personality preferences, work-style preferences, differences in strengths, attitudes, and approach—all are intertwined, and that can make for a rich but complex and uncomfortable discussion.

To do this work effectively requires that each of us be willing to truly consider alternative views, even to the point of abandoning our own, and to suspend our judgment, replacing it instead with curiosity. As you do this, ask clarifying, respectful questions of others. It's also important to ask yourself what you claim as your primary identity, relative to the group. Think also about ways in which your identity is similar to or different from the identity of others in the group.

Mainstreaming Cultural Curiosity

Cultural curiosity—the desire to learn and understand new cultures and people—is an essential key to success in global business and to navigating among our differences. People who are curious about others, and who maintain a desire to continuously learn, benefit enterprises by broadening their abilities to establish meaningful relationships. When we approach others in the spirit of inquiry, we open ourselves to making discoveries that support more significant innovation.

And just think about how much more fun work can be when curiosity, inquiry, and discovery are part of it! Mainstreaming cultural curiosity throughout a company brings enduring value to the people, the organization, its customers, and its suppliers.

Holidays and Observances

In this day and age, large companies commonly operate in global environments that require people to have some knowledge of cultural nuances, customs, and expectations of how to appropriately do business. We have the potential to interact with people of all different backgrounds, customs, and experiences. To be effective and relevant in navigating the differences among us, we need to include and be aware of cultural holidays, religious observations, and worldly celebrations from different parts of the globe.

Companies that intentionally celebrate—or, at a minimum, acknowledge—these holidays and observances help demonstrate both a commitment to cultural and other forms of diversity and show respect for the importance of building an awareness of the plentiful and wonderful differences among employees, leaders, and customers. This is a simple yet potentially meaningful way to create engagement and also mainstream the cultural curiosity in our workplaces.

To get you started, I've included links to two diversity calendars:

- www.diversitybestpractices.com/diversity-holidays-and-heritage-months

- www.jameswantstoknowyou.com/diversitycalendar/

Some celebrations may already be familiar to you. Many people, for instance, are aware that February is Black History Month. February is also the month to celebrate Chinese New Year, an important traditional holiday. Similarly, October is National Disability Employment Awareness Month. It's also LGBT History Month and Canadian Thanksgiving. Building understanding and awareness of the traditions and beliefs of others is a creative way to share the differences among people. Find out what your

coworkers and employees celebrate, ask them how they do it, and recognize it in a respectful, positive way.

Employee Resource Groups

Employee Resource Groups (ERGs) are groups of employees who regularly gather based on their shared identities, such as ethnicity, gender, race, sexual orientation, physical ability, military veteran status, and other characteristics. ERGs are sometimes also known as business resource groups, affinity groups, staff associations, or multicultural resource groups. Historically, these groups established themselves as social networks that primarily gathered outside the workplace so people could connect and nurture their shared identities. In more recent years, groups have transitioned; and through them, people work on initiatives with direct business impact, such as business development or recruiting.

Imagine a forward-thinking, progressive company that has whites and Asians learning the details of Black history, and men leading meaningful discussions about the value of the women's movement in American history. We could accomplish this in our companies by having executive sponsors of ERGs who are not the same demographic as the group being sponsored. When we do this, we create the substantive opportunity for a senior executive to learn about a different diversity dimension. That senior executive could then become a voice for the group at senior levels, among other company leaders who have the power and position to create organizational change.

To be able to successfully make this happen, the executive sponsor of a group would need to be someone who has:

- a commitment to learning

- a passion for the group
- a willingness to share with other executive sponsors
- the influence, power, and authority to support the ERG in question, help secure funding, host events, and provide executive-level support

Building on this, the subsequent cross-collaboration among executive sponsors would then create the opportunity for a forum through which people could share measurable results that showcase and strengthen the value of their various ERGs. Each group and its executive sponsor could also take advantage of opportunities for building cultural and identity awareness, which could help educate the rest of the workforce and build comfort with others who are different.

There are a few ways to form your own ERG. My advice is to first determine the purpose of the ERG—why it should exist, what its mission is, and what its goals are. Then, I suggest following the guidelines provided by the Human Rights Campaign (HRC). HRC guidelines are used to form LGBTI employee resource groups but can be used to help establish other ERGs for different populations. These guidelines recommend:

- examining any existing policies in your organization for forming ERGs
- making membership in the ERG open to everyone
- anticipating any negative reactions and how ERG leaders would handle possible objections to the formation or purpose of the group
- selecting an executive sponsor, someone with the influence, power, and authority to champion ERG plans to achieve goals and attain ongoing success

Navigating differences among people is hard to talk about and even harder to act on. But it is possible—and powerful—with dramatic benefits to the organizations that hold themselves accountable to this vital aspect of diversity and inclusion at work.

....

Quick Summary

Here are some key points to remember and questions to think about from this chapter:

- What happens outside work has a direct effect on employees at work. Silence among leaders and managers is often interpreted as people not caring.

- Determine the readiness of your organization before you broach sensitive topics.

- Learn the various intercultural conflict styles. Understand other cultures' norms and beliefs, as well as your own.

- Know yourself. Determine your readiness to lead conversations that shift thinking. Ask yourself:
  - Have I explored my unconscious biases?
  - Am I reasonably comfortable talking about difficult subjects?
  - Do I have meaningful relationships with diverse people and groups?
  - Do I have regular exposure to people who are different from me?
  - Do I have a high degree of emotional intelligence?
  - Do the people I lead trust me?
  - Do I trust myself?

- Abandon the assumption that what's good for you is good for others, since this can thwart movement toward mutual understanding.

- Explore and understand the multiple dimensions of diversity and inclusion.

- Leverage cultural holidays and Employee Resource Groups to build understanding of different groups and advance business goals.

- Learn from other leaders who communicate well about difficult topics.

- Avoid spontaneous conversations on polarizing topics. Instead, prepare for these in advance.

- Plan to have several conversations that build on one another. Learning to navigate difference is a process, not a one-time event!

Action Steps

Need to know how to apply what you just read? Here are some steps and ideas:

- Survey your employee base to measure the inclusiveness of the current workforce.
- Emotional intelligence (EQ) and conflict-management preferences matter greatly in a person's ability to do effective diversity and inclusion work; measure these.
- Conduct a cultural-competence inventory of your workforce using the Intercultural Development Inventory (IDI).

Continued

- Measure conflict-management styles of managers and leaders using the Thomas-Kilmann Instrument (TKI).
- Mainstream cultural curiosity by celebrating cultural holidays and establishing Employee Resource Groups (ERGs).
- Write your (mini) biography.
- Measure the cultural competence of your workforce and be transparent in sharing the results, along with actions for improvement.
- Develop cultural curiosity by writing and sharing brief biographies.
- Measure leadership inclusiveness.
- Conduct employee inclusion surveys. Act on the data you receive, establish a baseline, and then remeasure.
- Once organizational- and self-readiness are positively determined, you can begin the conversations!

CHAPTER FIVE

Measuring Results

No matter how beautiful the strategy,
one must occasionally look at results.

—WINSTON CHURCHILL

You've started the hard work of building up a diverse and inclusive workforce and creating an environment that embraces differences among its employees. You've begun to formulate a plan for continuing to educate and support people at all organizational levels. And you've communicated to people both inside and outside your organization that your company is going to champion diversity and inclusion. But to truly transform your organization, accountability matters, so you'll also need to come up with a plan for measuring and acting on the results.

It sounds analytical and maybe even a bit daunting, but think of this as simply finding a way to look at what you've done and gaining some perspective on it. This will allow you to not only see if the framework you've put in place is working but also make adjustments and tweaks as necessary. When you're able to objectively view the strengths, weaknesses, triumphs, and challenges of what you've set in motion, you'll be able to better assess how

your strategies can be more impactful, and then you can engage employees in a more active way.

In this chapter, I'll show you how to select metrics to guide your diversity and inclusion strategy and also provide you with examples of standard, innovative, and creative measures to consider. I'll make the case for open-book transparency—that is, the widespread sharing of results, both the good results and those needing improvement. And I'll suggest ways for you to make strategic course corrections so that you continue to improve while maintaining accountability for results.

How to Develop Metrics for Your Organization

Your number one goal in developing diversity and inclusion metrics is to create meaningful dialogue. You want your board of directors, executives, senior leaders, and their direct reports to have the best data possible to inform decisions on hiring, promotion, retention, cultural competence, and inclusive workplace climate. It's a time-consuming and costly mistake to get caught up in developing a complex set of metrics that will only confuse people and delay decision-making.

Keep it simple. Keep it concise. Link the metrics you select to the business goals of the organization. And put it all on a one-page dashboard for the company executives. This is the key to success with metrics (especially at the most senior levels).

> 66 *Don't get caught up in developing a complex set of metrics that will only confuse people and delay decision-making. Keep it simple. Keep it concise. Link the metrics you select to the business goals of the organization."*

The diversity and inclusion metrics you develop need to align with the goals you've established and also your organization's values. You want workplace diversity and inclusion to help you achieve heightened innovation, greater financial returns, and more engaged employees. But the purpose in advancing D&I in your company is to support not only your business but also the broader social well-being. As you develop the metrics for your organization, the focus needs to be both on quantitative measures—the number and percentage of people of color in senior roles, for example—and also on qualitative measures—which are used to evaluate the quality and results of your efforts on diversity and inclusion.

Create Metrics That Provide Useful Data

For metrics to be of value, you need to know employee demographics, baseline Equal Employment Opportunity (EEO) data. You'll need to track the number and percentage of women, men, Blacks, Latinos, Asians, persons with disabilities, LGBTI persons, and Native Americans at all organizational levels, including your board of directors. And you'll need to know year-over-year progress in hiring, promotions, and retention for each of the categories you are tracking.

You might also gather data on involuntary and voluntary turnover by age, race, gender, and ethnicity (including the reasons why, for those that exit, they are leaving or have been asked to leave), with the understanding that those voluntarily leaving may be reluctant to share the actual reasons for their decision.

I recommend beginning by taking an inventory of the data you currently capture—for example, the number of Blacks, Latinos, Asians, Native Americans, whites, and multiethnic people at each organizational level—and also looking at

segments of these ethnicities by gender and age. Next, create an inventory of data that you see value in having but which may not be captured, such as the number of veterans or persons with disabilities in your organization. Once you've inventoried the quantitative data, move on to the qualitative data and do the same, looking at the information you capture in employee surveys and through other instruments, as well as the data that is missing but desirable to have, like measures of cultural competence and inclusion.[1]

As you think about the metrics you're putting together, it's important to be sure you've covered a few critical areas:

- **Recruitment and representation metrics**—These look at the results of marketing to different candidates, new hires, workforce demographics, and attrition—all by race, ancestry (ethnicity), gender, age, veteran status, ability status, and sexual orientation. Recruitment and retention metrics answer questions like:
  - "If we set a goal to increase the percentage of Black women in senior leadership by 50%, did we achieve it?"
  - "What number and percentage of minority talent voluntarily left the organization in the past year?"

- **Talent development metrics**—These look at sponsorship and promotions and answer questions like:
  - "If we set a goal to promote 20% more people with disabilities, did we achieve it?"
  - "If we decided to assign executive sponsors to five senior-level women to champion their careers, did we accomplish that goal? And how have their careers progressed since sponsorship began?"

- **Supplier diversity metrics**—These look at direct contractor procurement and purchases from designated minority- and women-owned businesses, as well as those owned by LGBTI persons, veterans, and persons with disabilities. Calculate corporate spending with these groups and what you can do to help them succeed. These metrics answer questions like:
  - "Of the total amount of money we spent purchasing supplies in the past year, what percentage went to suppliers designated as women-owned, minority-owned, or veteran-owned businesses?"

- **Workplace climate metrics**—These look at how employees experience the organization and provide deeper insights than the quantitative metrics above. These measures come from worker satisfaction surveys, assessments of inclusivity, emotional intelligence (EQ), and cultural competence instruments. They answer questions like:
  - "How do employees perceive the benefits of diversity and inclusion programs?"
  - "Do employees feel like the company has a welcoming environment, with high levels of trust, transparency, and fairness?"
  - "What suggestions do employees have to improve diversity and inclusion in the organization?"
  - "What levels of cultural competence span the organization? And what actions can be taken to continuously improve?"

Think of the above categories as significant measurements on workforce diversity and inclusion. These metrics provide a solid combination of both quantitative and qualitative information to

get you started, and if acted upon, will move the organization in the right direction to achieve established D&I goals. They also help prepare senior leaders to move toward even more innovative and creative measures, which I'll discuss in the paragraphs that follow.

What Metrics Look Like

As I mentioned, the kind of metrics you develop will depend largely on the goals of your organization, where you are in the diversity and inclusion journey, and the progressiveness of your company leaders. You might use standard measures to establish a baseline if your organization is small and the D&I journey is just beginning.

As a new and growing company, your goal may be to simply measure year-over-year progress. But as your company advances in its D&I commitment and work, it's essential to move beyond baseline or standard measures and begin to also use external benchmarking to see how well you are performing. To do this, an organization determines who its competitors are relative to successful D&I (using data from the *DiversityInc* Top 50 survey, for example). Identifying companies that are achieving lofty goals in D&I provides an excellent basis for comparison as well as some potential learning opportunities. Often, these competitors are using more innovative and creative techniques to drive their success. I'll share more about these types of metrics next.

EXAMPLE #1: STANDARD MEASURES

To support the US Civil Rights Act (1964) and the Equal Employment Opportunity Act (1972), companies with 100 or more employees (and federal contractors with 50 or more) must file the government's Employer Information Report, commonly known as the EEO-1, annually. This is a mandatory report, which

provides a count of all employees by job category, ethnicity, race, and gender. EEO reports are designed to protect the civil rights of workers and look at employment patterns and representation to guard against overt discrimination.

For example, if a company reports that in the software engineering job category there are 1,000 white men, 3 Black men, and 10 women, this may indicate a recruitment, hiring, or retention disparity. In 2016, the Equal Employment Opportunity Commission (EEOC) proposed the addition of pay data and hours worked to the EEO report, to make it possible to spot pay discrimination and trends in working hours; but as of this writing, the proposal has not yet been enacted. Canada, Australia, many European countries, and some in South America have similar reporting structures in place.

Think of EEO measures as standard baseline reporting—numbers that tell you where your company stands and enable you to set goals for improvement or to advertise accomplishments. (Companies successful with diversity and inclusion are desirable organizations where many talented people want to work.) The intriguing thing about EEO reporting is that while it is mandatory to provide this information to the government, it is not required that companies publicly report this data.

Many organizations voluntarily do so, but for those companies that are not transparent in sharing this data openly, employees and potential new hires should ask: "Why not?" and request that senior leaders and managers begin sharing this information.

EXAMPLE #2: INNOVATIVE MEASURES

If you have been implementing strategies for diversity and inclusion in your workforce for a while and are ready to delve deeper into measuring effectiveness, then consider a powerful approach

recently described in *Harvard Business Review*[2] and titled "To Understand Whether Your Company Is Inclusive, Map How Your Employees Interact" as your next step in the journey to more effective D&I.

Organizational network analysis (ONA) is a method for studying and visualizing how people communicate with one another in an organization. ONA is a fairly new and highly innovative way for companies to ascertain just how inclusive they genuinely are. This mapping technique produces a chart showing the human interaction among individuals in specific networks or groups.

At a high level, here's how it works: let's say you've accomplished the work of hiring a diverse set of employees. You know that the ability to retain your workers involves creating an environment where they feel welcomed and valued, where their contributions matter and opportunities for advancing exist. You want to map how workers interact in order to determine if your company is truly inclusive. So you ask each person in a designated group questions like "Who do you turn to most frequently when you need help with a critical decision?" and "Who in this company do you believe would stand up for you during a difficult time?"[3] The people named are then asked to identify colleagues they turn to for help and those they trust to support them. This data enables a company to see if the relationships have mutual trust and respect.

By expanding the network analysis and adding additional people (and questions), the company stands to discover whether or not unconscious biases may be driving specific behaviors. For example, do men seek help with critical decisions from women or primarily from other men? A host of discoveries about inclusive behaviors is possible using organizational network analysis. However, most organizations are not skilled in the type of complexity management that an ONA requires. Fortunately, there are excellent

consultants with this expertise, including Rob Cross (robcross.org/research/what-is-ona/) and Deloitte's Human Capital consulting practice (www2.deloitte.com/us/en/pages/human-capital/articles/organizational-network-analysis.html).

EXAMPLE #3: CREATIVE MEASURES

Organizations in the earlier stages of their D&I journeys implement standard metrics. And companies with mature D&I programs focused on continuous improvement may progressively undertake an organizational network analysis. You may be wondering if there are other measures to consider, creative approaches that any company may benefit from using. The answer is "yes." Here are a few examples:

- **Amount of exposure to senior management**—Companies send a message that they value the contributions of certain employees by providing them with high-visibility work assignments. Take a look at who is assigned "special projects" and the senior leaders supporting them. Measure the diversity of these partnerships.

- **Reverse mentoring programs**—There's a tendency to think of younger employees learning from older workers, but the reverse can also be true. Start pilot programs to test and measure the value of partnerships among employees of different generations.

- **Executive and senior-level compensation**—Link the achievement of robust diversity and inclusion goals to incentive compensation. Each year, take a look to see if everyone is attaining the maximum. This data will show if D&I is taken seriously at the most senior levels.

❝ *Organizations measure the things they care about.* ”

Whether the diversity and inclusion measures a company takes are standard, innovative, creative, or some combination of the three, the critical thing is that metrics are created. Organizations measure the things they care about. Generating actionable D&I data to support your business strategy sends a message to employees, suppliers, potential new hires, and the community that a company is serious about its commitment to doing the hard work of developing diversity and enhancing inclusion.

How to Read the Results

Measurement is really about understanding. Remember that one goal in developing D&I metrics is to support a dialogue among senior leaders. Once you've been able to gather some numbers or obtain some information about employee perceptions of diversity and inclusion, you'll want to use that information to tell a story. This is the story of where your organization currently stands, what the numbers say, and how the people feel. Analyze the data and categorize it based on good outcomes, poor outcomes, and outcomes that need improvement. Compare the actual data with goals you are targeting. Did you achieve your goals? Why or why not? Ask for any clarification you need on messages. And check that your interpretation is sound. Combine the data into a storyboard that you will share broadly within the company.

❝ *Measurement is really about understanding. The information you gather tells the story of where your organization currently stands, what the numbers say, and how people in your company feel.* ”

And if, for example, your metrics point to the fact that you have a decrease in the number of minority employees versus the increase you strove to attain, share this information, your disappointment with it, why you think it occurred, and the steps you will take—and perhaps want all employees to take—to remedy it in a specific timeframe. Bad news does not improve with age, and people appreciate honesty, especially from senior leaders.

How to Share Your Findings

Many companies boast about being "metrics-driven" but fail to provide metrics around the gender and race pay gap, or the lack thereof. Even if they've collected the data, very little in their organizations can change unless they make their findings known to employees. It's worth noting that the leading firms in the *DiversityInc* Top 50 Companies annual survey are companies that voluntarily run gender and race pay gap numbers and share their data internally. And the countries of Austria, Belgium, and Great Britain have laws requiring companies of a certain size—typically 250 or more employees—to report their data on gender pay inequity publicly.

I can't emphasize enough the importance of sharing the findings of your metrics. I've seen firsthand the way in which enterprises that share their data with employees and work to fix the gap are the ones that ultimately prove themselves to be inclusive organizations people want to be and stay a part of. If you want to take steps to turn your company into a truly diverse and inclusive one, you'll want to share your data.

Remember the inclusion scores and the cultural competence measures discussed in chapter four? Share these. Break the inclusion scores down by department or work area (teams of ten or more), and plan for dialogue with the people who provided the

data. There are few messages worse sending to your employees than when you ask for their input and then ignore it after they offer it. At a minimum, you should share what you received, what you heard and learned, and most importantly, what you plan to do with the findings. More than anything, remember to also listen well so that your people feel and know that they matter to you.

> 66 *Share the input you received, what you heard and learned, and most importantly, what you plan to do with the findings. Remember to also listen well so that your people feel and know that they matter to you.*"

Open-Book Transparency

As you will share these metrics beyond the executive level, it's helpful to remember that open communication is a double-edged sword. When you don't tell people what's going on, they imagine the worst. This is as true in business as in life. If your child is supposed to be home by 10:00 p.m. and you haven't heard from him, your mind might go to "My kid could be lying dead in a ditch by the side of the road," or some other extreme sentiment.

The same thing happens at work. When companies in the tech industry refused to disclose their EEO numbers, people assumed they had something to hide. That turned out to be the truth; they had embarrassing numbers to protect. If a boss isn't openly sharing what's going on, workers might naturally imagine that there's something terrible to hide—perhaps the business outlook is worse than they feared, and layoffs are coming.

On the flip side of that, when you tell people what's going on, it often serves to validate at least some of their fears. Given the options—to share or not to share—it's better to share. Being

transparent with information is vital when you're building an inclusive work environment, because transparency builds and maintains trust. It also creates an excellent platform for sensitive discussions that wouldn't typically occur if the workplace culture were different, like discussions about pay equity relative to race, gender, and experience (age).

Data related to race, gender, age, sexual orientation, and other factors is quite reasonably seen as sensitive information. It's best to share diversity and inclusion metrics in person. The company board of directors and senior leadership teams are best served with a one-page dashboard to review. Mid-level managers and staff can often absorb more data, though it's important to not overwhelm any group with too much information. Instead, try focusing employees on the story the data tells, an understanding of why, and the plan to improve. You can invite input and suggestions; there may be interpretations people haven't yet thought of.

And remember to celebrate successes, because this is not easy work. So recognize and praise any of your accomplishments in advancing women, minorities, and other extraordinary people.

How to Hold People Accountable

After you have a plan in place, communicate this to everyone in the company. It's human nature for things to return to the status quo, so you and company leaders will need to agree to hold everyone—including yourselves—accountable.

As mentioned earlier, one way to establish accountability is to tie compensation to diversity goals. This is particularly important at the executive levels but can also descend to middle managers as well. In addition, it can be useful to show progress and challenges

over time by updating and publishing progress charts on a quarterly basis, adjusting these based on the size of your company. And ensure that your engagement indexes, which are a composite of your company's inclusion scores and cultural responsiveness from your survey data, are updated at least annually. This will provide you with progress reports over time that serve to complement and explain the challenges and accomplishments the company has had year after year. It tells your organization's story relative to diversity and inclusion.

Complex Problems Often Have Simple Solutions

In my experience, it's extremely difficult to shift an organizational environment toward inclusivity without first using metrics to take a baseline measure and find out where a company stands. Having spent a decade working for a global management and technology consulting firm, interacting with multiple clients in different industries, and then working for another decade in healthcare, I've seen the way people dismiss problems, assigning the blame and accountability to someone else.

I've sat on many executive committees where, for example, we've discussed the issue of pay equity, and though everyone acknowledges the problem, company leaders will often believe the matter belongs to someone else. "This is wrong," I've heard them say. "We certainly don't treat our employees that way." The discussions are always overwhelmingly and notably short. In their view, somehow it's always the "other guy" or someone else who's causing the problem. I cannot recall a single instance over the span

of my career when actual data—numbers, facts, testimonials from employees—was presented or discussed to either validate or invalidate the issue.

To me, the solution is incredibly simple. Run the numbers. And not just to figure out what the pay gaps are for women versus men. Let's look at race. Are Black men paid the same as white men for doing the same job? What about Latinas? Disabled persons?

Metrics are important. They can point out the obvious. They offer a way we can take a large, seemingly insurmountable problem, identify it, hold people accountable for it, and do something about it. Complex problems can have simple solutions.

Quick Summary

Here are some key points to remember from this chapter:

- Metrics matter. Tracking and sharing data with transparency builds trust in a company's senior leaders and holds everyone accountable for achieving diversity and inclusion targets at all levels.

- Simplicity is important. Use a one-page dashboard to tell the story of D&I to executive leaders.

- Diversity and inclusion metrics may be standard, innovative, creative, or some combination of the three.

- Even with sensitive data, it's better to share D&I results than not to share.

- Thank people for contributing to employee climate surveys and follow up with what's been learned and what will be done next. Don't ask for feedback if you aren't prepared to acknowledge it and take action.

- Achieving targets in some categories does not mean your work is done. Set goals for year-over-year improvement. Then begin using external benchmarks to understand the competitive value of your progress.

- Success with diversity and inclusion makes you a desired company to work for *and* buy from. Advertise this success!

Action Steps

Need to know how to apply what you just read? Here are some steps and ideas:

- Inventory the data you have and the data you want. Use both quantitative and qualitative measures.

- After gathering data, interpret it to determine the story it tells.

- Decide on actions to take based on data and feedback—and execute!

CONCLUSION

Bringing It All Together

Diversity fatigue means we've momentarily lost sight of the magnitude of opportunity before us.

—BARBARA ADAMS

Increasingly, businesses are recognizing the tremendous strategic value of having diverse, inclusive workforces. They know the benefits are strong, well documented, and positive. But the slow progress of change has been palpable, and we've all seen and experienced the resulting frustrations. We hear talk of "diversity fatigue," something that exemplifies the conundrum to approaches that just haven't produced sustainable results.

Forward-thinking, progressive leaders understand that it's time for us to bravely explore new ways to make this work. Change *is possible*, but as I mentioned, the job ahead is hard and not for the faint of heart. It's for those of us willing to develop a new narrative and stride down the path to attain a workplace in which differences among people not only abound but also are leveraged for the betterment of individuals, companies, and society.

My goal with this book is to equip and empower you to reframe your thinking, to shift your mindset, and to give you

boldness and clarity so you can deliver on the promise of inclusive diversity. Through the progression of ideas, I've tried to provide some beginning steps and show you what's at stake. Let's bring it all together here and see how this might inform you as you come up with an action plan you can apply to your organization. Here are some of the important take-aways:

Chapter One Take-Aways: Acknowledging the Problem, Embracing the Opportunity

In chapter one, you learned how the lack of diversity in technology and in other industries is still a problem that exists today, even after fifty years of laws, policies, regulations, and education and training programs were put in place to eradicate prejudice and discrimination. As you think about how to tackle the problem of lack of diversity in your own company and industry, recognize that the issue is two-fold:

- Unless boards of directors, company leaders, and individual employees have belief systems that work inclusively, a diverse, inclusive workplace can never truly develop. It starts with people. It starts with a change in thinking and a change of heart. We might put together a powerful business case and have systems in place for recruiting, hiring, and retaining diverse workforces, but all of this really is secondary to people's belief systems. Create an environment that supports new thinking and requires surfacing the hidden biases that drive behavior and actions to shift those preferences by making contact with others who are different from us.

- Beyond acknowledging the problem of homogeneous workplaces, it's vital to create opportunities that set our companies up for success. Redesigning work environments and organizational charts are easy ways to begin. Examining assumptions, recognizing the role of emotion in decision-making, and providing safe spaces to discuss the systems of oppression that have brought us to this place are much harder.

It might be overwhelming to think of the magnitude of the problem. But I firmly believe we have an opportunity here. Though real change doesn't come easily, I've seen it happen. The opportunity we have is in our recognition that human logic and emotion are complicated things that become intertwined in business and life, so as much as we'd like to be able to, we need to understand that we can't use rational thought alone to overcome the challenge of diversity and inclusion.

Enough research data exists, however, for companies to be able to calculate the cost of the status quo, develop a business case for D&I, and bring it to the board of directors. Then companies can leverage a senior-level chief diversity & inclusion officer (CDIO) to lead the efforts of implementing the behavioral interventions that are necessary to prime desirable behavior and help everyone in the organization acknowledge unconscious bias, develop cultural curiosity, and recognize the power of self-reflection.

We all possess the ability to learn to replace the judgment and bias that naturally occur in us with curiosity about differences. And that is truly the beginning of embracing the opportunity that lies in workforce diversity and inclusion.

Chapter Two Take-Aways:
Reframing Your Thinking

Organizational culture is akin to the speed of light, in that neither changes. Stop reaching for culture change—because it isn't going to happen. *Behaviors* can change, however, so I recommend focusing on this, which is in and of itself challenging enough.

Remember that reframing our thinking requires that we adjust our personal mindsets to understand that we're all born into and deeply influenced by a structural institution, that unconscious biases lead us to do things that run counter to our professed beliefs, and that neuroscience can help us process why this is and alleviate a sense of guilt so that we can begin adjusting the way we think about people who are different from us. It also enables us to understand that the idea of meritocracy is not only fictional but also something holding us back from success, and it needs to be abandoned.

Often, and if compelling enough, a change in the way we think leads to a change in the way we act. Reframing the way we think takes practice, awareness, and intention. But as you work to become a cultural detective and develop curiosity about differences, you will be thinking more for yourself and writing mental prescriptions that greatly help. Ultimately, as you act with mindful intention, you elevate yourself and others. Just know that the work is hard, gets easier with practice, and produces rewards that benefit everyone.

Chapter Three Take-Aways:
Making a Plan Like No Other

To transform a homogeneous organization into one that is both diverse and inclusive mandates a creative reengineering of recruitment, hiring, engagement, and performance management.

Companies need to wave the white flag on the "war on talent" and start building talent instead of always trying to buy it from just a few feeder pool sources.

Your company can also learn to hire holistically. Remember that although IQ may predict SAT scores, SAT scores don't predict job performance or success in life. This is because fluid intelligence and crystalized intelligence both matter. So when we hire across the chasms of gender, age, and race, this is how we'll get true diversity of thought and experience in our organizations.

Companies need to also stop saying they would hire women and minorities but that the qualified candidates are just "not there." Organizations that do this are, whether they realize it or not, playing the victim; and this has hurt business, individuals, society, and our global economy. We need to not just think differently but *do* differently. And this requires that we practice.

Take action to prevent interviewer bias. Use virtual and augmented reality to help employees understand how it *feels* to be different in an organization. Practice holistic hiring. Use appreciative inquiry. Look beyond knowledge, skills, and abilities (KSAs) to identify the key *values* someone effectively needs for a job. We need to realize that we can find the people we need to hire because they are everywhere. The results we want and need can only come when we intentionally draw upon the courage to hire differently. Remember that the so-called bar and who clears it says more about a company and its hiring practices than about the candidates applying for a given role. As you change processes to hire better and acquire more women, older workers, and minorities, practice *valuing* these important workers. That's the first step on the path to retaining them.

Our current performance management systems are really about forced distribution rankings that hinder diversity. We are

long overdue for a change. Innovation comes through collaboration, not through a grading-on-a-curve, old-school, competitive, identify-the-"high-potentials" model. It's time to start developing a performance ecosystem that's kept in balance by a genuine diversity of talent.

In *Business @ the Speed of Thought,* Bill Gates writes, "As we look ahead into the century, leaders will be those who empower others."[1] Implicit in those words are essential qualities of inclusive leaders, people who we trust will both work for the common good and share their success, people who view their roles as both a responsibility and a privilege. These are men and women who serve, listen, learn, engage, and optimize their own physical and emotional health to maintain their energy for caring for their employees. They are proficient in the art of humble inquiry and able to create environments that all employees want to be a part of. They embrace the behaviors of inclusive leaders and practice with authenticity.

Chapter Four Take-Aways: Learning to Navigate Difference

Meaningful conversations about diversity are not for the faint of heart. Talking about race, gender, sexual orientation, religion, and other social differences and perspectives in a work group can cause discomfort, and this can lead to a lack of trust, concern about disrespect, and potential for interpersonal conflict. So when we create the time and space for these types of meaningful conversations, we must be prepared to manage the situations.

Done well, however, the opportunities for employees to interact with mixed-perspective groups also give them the chance to consider alternate views, experiences, and thoughts they might not otherwise have had. Remember that the time it takes for

each person to feel that they've truly been listened to and heard is invaluable for creating the kind of inclusivity and understanding of difference that spurs amazing performance in an organization.

To do this work effectively requires that each of us be willing to truly consider alternative views, even to the point of abandoning our own and suspending our judgment enough to replace it with curiosity.

Also, it's easy to forget that what happens outside work often has a direct effect on what happens inside work. Issues involving social justice are in the news daily; and when these occur, silence among company leaders and managers about some of these important issues implies a lack of caring. It's crucial that we engage at these times. But rather than spontaneously diving in, we need to approach these situations carefully.

Before we even begin to broach sensitive topics, we need to first have taken steps to determine the readiness of our organization. We can do this by learning the various intercultural conflict styles and understanding other cultures' norms and beliefs, as well as our own. It's important that we know ourselves. Then we can better determine our readiness to lead the tough but good conversations that shift thinking and enact change.

It's important to also remember that even as we normalize these types of conversations in our workplaces, we need to be careful about avoiding spur-of-the-moment conversations on polarizing topics. The best thing we can do in these instances is prepare in advance. I recommend planning to have *several* conversations that build on one another, because having meaningful, bold conversations that shift thinking is a process, not a one-time event.

    66 *Having meaningful, bold conversations that shift thinking is a process, not a one-time event."*

As we engage with our workforce, we must learn to lean into discomfort and practice becoming curious about people who are different from us. We need to mainstream cultural curiosity throughout our company. I recommend issuing an Inclusion Survey—I've included a sample for you on pages 154–156—and a Cultural Responsiveness Survey (Intercultural Development Inventory) to invite employees into the conversation and help them determine their areas of strengths and weaknesses in the company. Then, we need to make sure we follow up on our survey results.

Remember that employees are far more likely to stay in an organization in which they have meaningful work, feel valued by leaders, managers, and peers for their contributions, and can be their authentic selves at work. It behooves companies to create environments that embrace values of honesty, genuineness, and difference, and to actively work to eliminate behaviors that run counter to principles of psychological safety.

Chapter Five Take-Aways: Measuring Results

The most senior leadership of our organization needs a simple, clear set of metrics that can be read on a one-page dashboard. In the name of transparency, these measures should be shared company-wide and need to link directly to business goals. Companies should select what's relevant and what a new executive could interpret if seeing the chart for the first time. We also need to be sure to include some measures to show progress over the years and some external benchmarking measures as well. That's it. The key is to resist the temptation to show everything, going overboard with complexity.

Next, organizations will need to obtain metrics in four critical areas:

- The pipeline, which looks at recruiting, new hires, workforce demographics, and attrition—all by race, ethnicity, gender, age, and so on.

- Talent development, which looks at sponsorship and promotions as well as self- and team-development offerings and outcomes.

- Senior-level commitment to D&I, including the diverse make-up of the top three to four organizational levels, beginning with the board of directors. This also includes a commitment to accountability measures, such as compensation linked to diversity results from established goals.

- Supplier diversity metrics that include direct contractor procurement and purchases from designated minority- and women-owned businesses, LGBTI-owned suppliers, and suppliers owned by persons with disabilities and veterans. We'll want to calculate corporate spending with these groups and what we can do to help them succeed.

Once we have the data, we must share, share, share with our workforce and communicate our results widely. We need to thank individuals and groups appropriately and be certain that any survey data employees were asked to participate in (such as inclusion and cultural responsiveness surveys) is shared with them in a safe, collegial, welcoming environment.

Final Thoughts

Any company that wants to succeed in creating and sustaining a healthy, diverse, inclusive workforce can do so. This book offers you

a new path to success. Only those companies with progressive-thinking boards of directors and action-oriented senior leaders have a chance at succeeding in developing the mindset required to carry out this work. Those that do succeed, however, will not only benefit from the enhanced business innovation that diverse, inclusive workforces bring but also be positively affecting the social fabric of humanity.

Organizations are complex systems, and major change is anxiety-provoking. But I am hopeful. As of this writing, there are 330 corporate and academic leaders who have signed a CEO Action for Diversity & Inclusion pledge.[2] This is a commitment to have the unusual, often challenging conversations necessary in order to support diverse environments. It's a commitment to creating safe spaces, expanding education and awareness of hidden bias, developing people holistically, and also, importantly, publishing the results of their actions. These leaders recognize the strong need for more seats at the table and new behaviors to ensure that every voice is heard. They understand that there is more to gain from a greater participation of women and under-represented minorities than from like-minded thinking. They know that *everyone* benefits from the enormous potential of diverse, inclusive environments.

I am hopeful that their actions will disrupt the status quo. They will face some difficult moments. This work is not easy. But their collective commitment is a powerful start, and if this book can help them achieve results on this important journey, then I am humbled and grateful to be of service.

Acknowledgments

When I began mulling over the idea for this book three years ago, I needed to solicit input, suggestions, and perspectives to move forward. I am indebted to some generous people who took the time to read early drafts and provide feedback and encouragement to keep going. I want to acknowledge Sumayyah Emeh Edu, Judith Poirier, NaKeia Warren, May Jones, Lisa Clark Keith, Yesmina Zavala, Lisa M. Young, Ava Annette Newman, and Linda Jay. Thank you for your honesty, ideas, and belief in this work. I am grateful to you. Thank you, Karen Banas, Carolyn Kellams, and Kate Lynch, for your ongoing confidence in me. And a special thank you to my brother, William Banas, for retweeting every diversity and inclusion comment I post.

A gift from the universe came my way in the form of my editor, Jessica Choi, without whom this work would not be the product it is today. Thank you, Jessica, for your probing questions, ideas for expansion and clarification, and enthusiasm for this topic. Working with you made a long process joyful. I am fortunate to have the supporting talent of Tanya Hall, Jen Glynn, Justin Branch, Chantel Stull, and all the excellent folks at Greenleaf Book Group Publishers. I thank you all. I also want to recognize Hobbs Allison for first advocating about the value of this work and for the periodic prompts and check-ins. You and Justin have a gift for the gentle nudge. My appreciation further extends

to Elizabeth Brown, for both your copyedits and your enthusiastic reader reactions, which were delightful to receive.

My gratitude also goes to Peggy Grant, PhD, for her exemplary demonstration of how to facilitate meaningful conversations about diversity. You are an exceptional teacher, Dr. Grant. I thank Helen Archer-Duste for mentorship, and Ronald Copeland, MD, for suggesting the need for a framework to navigate difference. Mary-Frances Winters's work about how to talk about race and other polarizing topics at work informed my own. I value your gift for communication. My appreciation goes to Valerie Batts, PhD, for a chart to simplify differences, and to Robert Sachs, PhD, for the opportunity to meet Mahzarin Banaji in person. Thank you to the members of my Mastermind group—Jim Prost, Gloria Dunn-Violin, Don McCrea, and Millie Anderson—for your continuous, enthusiastic encouragement and valuable ideas. Hugs and thanks to Corinne Adams and Amelia for providing periodic fun distractions that kept me energized along the way. I also want to recognize and thank the 2013–2014 staff of Kaiser Permanente's National Diversity & Inclusion Department for a valuable learning journey. Finally, I thank my clients, past and present, for your commitment and courage in making the promise of inclusive diversity a reality in your organizations. You own the future.

Frequently Asked Questions

When I give speeches, deliver workshops, or provide educational consulting services to organizations, I like to allow time for questions from the audience. The following questions come up with some regularity, so in anticipation that readers may wonder about these topics, I thought I'd share them, along with my answers.

Companies should hire the best person for the job. Period. Isn't hiring for diversity just "lowering the bar"?

The concern about "lowering the bar" stems from an incorrect and biased belief that a company has designed and implemented a so-called high bar that enables them to identify and hire only the "best" people. It is sometimes used as a misguided excuse to explain the reason that more women and minorities aren't hired—because they aren't able to meet that high bar.

In reality, many companies have antiquated, poorly designed hiring processes that fail to adequately evaluate highly qualified and often diverse candidates. By relying on selection processes that are at odds with research on how to most effectively evaluate people, companies make decisions based on hidden biases and on information that isn't relevant to the jobs for which they're hiring.

Organizations interested in hiring more women and diverse

candidates need not lower the bar; rather, they should challenge themselves to raise the bar. Companies can use a host of new technologies that take bias out of the selection process. Interview processes can be redesigned to have the hiring manager actively look for valuable differences in candidates. Job applicants deemed "not a culture fit" should require a clear, succinct, written, rational explanation by the interviewer of what *exactly* is meant. Anything not defensible using critical thinking and the absence of bias should be disregarded. Look up the most current, progressive approaches to hiring women and minority candidates and use them to get results.

If diverse companies outperform non-diverse companies, then how do you explain the success of Apple, Facebook, and Google?

Money is equated with power, and all of these companies are profit generators for their investors. They are seen as successful when based primarily on this measure. Look closer, however, and you'll learn that they are also driven by algorithms recently discovered to be widely infected by human bias.[1] Apply some critical thinking to the definition of success, and the effects of these companies on the human condition become less than stellar.

Google and Facebook make the majority (over 90%) of their revenue from advertising. They're not great product companies; they are ad pushers. And Apple's fate is uncertain given the saturation of smartphones in the market. All have been called out for hostile work cultures that are particularly demeaning to women and underrepresented minorities. If we stop worshiping at the altar of profit generation as *the* measure of success, then we could reasonably ask: How much better and broader would

their products, services, and organizational structures be had they embraced diversity from inception? Detroit was once unstoppable, too. We know what happened there.

Does it seem that Americans in general are afraid to have real conversations on taboo topics like race, diversity, and inequality?

I was in China a couple of years ago, traveling with a very funny African-American man and a few others as part of a school group. The two of us were quite popular wherever we went—me with my blonde hair and blue eyes and him with his dark skin and broad smile. The Chinese stopped us constantly for photographs. They were delighted to meet others who looked so different from them. We split up at times and began an informal contest of sorts, to see who was the more popular. He won after announcing in a crowd that he was "Obama's brother," which was not true! I remember feeling struck by how much our "differences" were framed as a good thing, something to be curious and happy about. Now, to the question . . .

"Americans" in general are an awfully broad group, but my sense is that there is a hesitancy to have meaningful conversations about race, diversity, inequality, sex, money, and a host of other "sensitive" topics. Puritan roots of early colonial times influence behavioral norms now, even centuries later. That said, having real conversations on these topics doesn't come naturally to most people. This is based on learned behavior.

I'm personally encouraged by the heightened level of conversation, especially around diversity, and the commitment to action that some leaders are taking. But in the end, it is only results that count, and we've still got quite a long way to go.

Our company is expanding internationally, and our diversity officer talks about "cultural context." What is the meaning of "cultural context"?

Let's say I am in the United States and someone asks for my business card. It is perfectly appropriate for me to reach into my pocket and casually hand this person my card. The person asking knows that my contact information is on the card, and it would seem inappropriately self-important for me to make a big deal of the request or call attention to the card. So I thank this person for asking and offer the card.

Now, let's say I'm in China and someone asks for my business card. It is expected that I will, with both hands, formally present my card to the person making the request. And it is expected that I will receive this person's card with the same formality. The card is seen as an extension of the person and should be treated respectfully. The card is seen as an extension of the person and should be treated respectfully.

So, same request, very different responses. This is cultural context.

Cultural context looks at the society that individuals are raised in and how their culture affects behavior. It incorporates learned values and shared attitudes among groups of people. It includes language, norms, customs, ideas, beliefs, and meanings. This is why before traveling to a foreign country, it is helpful to learn about the culture of a country and its people, so that your behaviors can be placed in context while visiting.

APPENDIX TWO

Critical Skills to Consider in Workforce Hiring, Development, and Planning

As I mentioned in chapter three, we need to consider the hard and soft skills that will serve our companies well as we strategically build, grow, and develop our workforces. The following lists critical skills that the Institute for the Future in Palo Alto, California, researched and compiled in its profoundly useful *Future Work Skills 2020* report. (Visit www.iftf.org/futureworkskills/ to read the full report.) Authors Anna Davies, Devin Fidler, and Marina Gorbis identified, among others, these skills:

- **The ability to determine the deeper meaning or significance of what is being expressed**—Machines make poor thinkers, despite the best advances in artificial intelligence. This is largely due to the inability of artificial intelligence to understand context in language. Machines aren't good at making sense of data; people are. Yet biases are input from human to machine. Machines cannot identify these biases; only humans can surface and bring awareness to hidden prejudice.

- **The ability to connect to others in a deep and direct way, to sense and stimulate reactions and desired interactions**—For machines, feeling and emotion are just as complex as making sense of data. The best advances in

robotics are not bringing us much closer. Employees with a strong emotional quotient (EQ) are vital to collaboration and relationship-making within a company.

- **Proficiency at thinking and coming up with solutions and responses beyond those that are rote or rule-based—** The ability to quickly and creatively respond to unique, unexpected circumstances will require novel thinking and adaptability.

- **The ability to operate in different cultural settings—** Corporate progress is enhanced by the collective differences of many employees. Companies *see* diversity as a driver of innovation. But that is not the same as working toward the reality.

- **The ability to translate vast amounts of data into abstract concepts and to understand data-based reasoning—** Computational thinking skills will be required and the use of simulations will become a core expertise.

- **The ability to critically assess and develop content that uses new media forms, and to leverage those media for persuasive communication—**Communications are moving from static, slide-based approaches to dynamic, real-time, visual approaches. Workers will need to become fluent in these new approaches and must be able to assess and interpret them.

- **Literacy in and ability to understand concepts across multiple disciplines—**Multidisciplinary approaches to solving increasingly complex problems are helpful. Transdisciplinary approaches, which involve a depth of knowledge in

one field *and* the capacity to converse in a broader range of disciplines, are even more desirable.

- **The ability to represent and develop tasks and work processes for desired outcomes**—Designing and planning environments so that they are maximally conducive to the outcomes desired is becoming a must.

- **The ability to discriminate and filter information for importance, and to understand how to maximize cognitive functioning by using a variety of tools and techniques**—Information overload leads to cognitive overload. Developing tools to reduce the stress that comes with feeling overwhelmed and simplifying data to maximize its usefulness will be skills of immense value.

- **The ability to work productively, drive engagement, and demonstrate presence as a member of a virtual team**—Creating environments where others feel present and available, but where an individual can also focus on the task at hand, will be increasingly valued and needed in the global workspace.

References

Alter, A. 2012. *Drunk Tank Pink: and Other Unexpected Forces That Shape How We Think, Feel, and Behave.* New York: Penguin Press.

Babbie, E. 1998. *The Practice of Social Research.* Belmont, CA: Wadsworth Publishing.

Banaji, M. R., and Greenwald, A. G. 2013. *Blindspot: Hidden Biases of Good People.* New York: Delacorte Press.

Bennett, M. W. 2010. "Unraveling the Gordian Knot of Implicit Bias in Jury Selection: The Problems of Judge-Dominated Voir Dire, the Failed Promise of Batson, and Proposed Solutions." *Harvard Law and Policy Review,* vol. 4, no. 1 (Winter), 149–171.

Blankenship, K. M., Bray, S. J., and Merson, M. H. 2000. "Structural Interventions in Public Health." *AIDS* 2000, vol. 14, Suppl. 1, S11–S12.

Bock, L. 2015. *Work Rules! Insights from Inside Google That Will Transform How You Live and Lead.* New York: Hachette Book Group.

Brizendine, L. 2006. *The Female Brain.* New York: Broadway Books.

Brizendine, L. 2010. *The Male Brain.* New York: Broadway Books.

Buckingham, M., and Goodall, A. 2015. "Reinventing Performance Management." *Harvard Business Review.* hbr. org/2015/04/reinventing-performance-management.

Cain, S. 2013. *Quiet: The Power of Introverts in a World That Can't Stop Talking.* New York: Broadway Books.

Catalyst. 2013. *High Potentials in the Pipeline: On Their Way to the Boardroom.*

Chua, A., and Rubenfeld, J. 2014. *The Triple Package: How Three Unlikely Traits Explain the Rise and Fall of Cultural Groups in America.* New York: Penguin Press.

Colfax, R., Rivera, J., and Perez, K. 2010. "Applying Emotional Intelligence (EQ-I) in the Workplace: Vital to Global Business Success." *Journal of International Business Research*, Suppl. 1 (Special Issue 1), 89–98.

Cottrell, J. 2014. "What would it look like if . . . Recruitment and hiring were productive and fun?" *AICommons.* https://appreciativeinquiry.champlain.edu/wp-content/uploads/2017/10/Appreciative-Inquiry-in-the-recruitment-and-hiring-of-new-employees.pdf.

Davies, A., Fidler, D., and Gorbis, M. 2011. *Future Work Skills 2020.* Institute for the Future: University of Phoenix Research Institute, Palo Alto, CA. www.iftf.org.

Detert, J. R., and Edmondson, A. C. 2011. "Implicit Voice Theories: Taken-for-Granted Rules of Self-Censorship at Work." *Academy of Management Journal*, vol. 54, 461–476.

Eagleman, D. 2011. *Incognito: The Secret Lives of the Brain.* New York: Vintage Books.

Edmondson, A. C. 1999. "Psychological Safety and Learning Behavior in Work Teams." *Administrative Science Quarterly*, vol. 44, 350–383.

Edmondson, A. C. 2012. *Teaming: How Organizations Learn, Innovate, and Compete in the Knowledge Economy*. San Francisco: Jossey-Bass Publishers.

Employers Network for Equality and Inclusion. 2014. "Disability: A Research Study on Unconscious Bias." shiftelt.com/wp-content/uploads/2017/04/SHIFT-Unconscious-Bias-White-Pape.pdf.

Ferdman, B. M., and Deane, B. R. 2014. *Diversity at Work: The Practice of Inclusion*. San Francisco: Jossey-Bass.

Flinders, C. L. 2002. *The Values of Belonging: Rediscovering Balance, Mutuality, Intuition, and Wholeness in a Competitive World*. San Francisco: HarperCollins.

Frost, S. 2014. *The Inclusion Imperative: How Real Inclusion Creates Better Business and Builds Better Societies*. Philadelphia: Kogan Page Limited.

Gabriel, S., and Gardner, W. L. 1999. "Are There 'His' and 'Hers' Types of Interdependence? The Implications of Gender Differences in Collective versus Relational Interdependence for Affect, Behavior, and Cognition." *Journal of Personality and Social Psychology*, vol. 77, no. 3, 642–655. dx.doi.org/10.1037/0022-3514.77.3.642.

Gallos, J. V. (Ed.). 2006. *Organization Development: A Jossey-Bass Reader*. San Francisco: Jossey-Bass.

Gates, W. H. III. 1999. *Business @ the Speed of Thought*. New York: Warner Books.

Gladwell, M. 2005. *Blink: The Power of Thinking Without Thinking*. New York: Hachette Book Group.

Gould, S. J. 1996. *The Mismeasure of Man*, rev. ed. New York: W. W. Norton & Company.

Grant Thornton International Business Report. 2016. *Women in Senior Management: Setting the Stage for Growth.*

Gray, J. 2012. *Men Are from Mars, Women Are from Venus: The Classic Guide to Understanding the Opposite Sex.* New York: Harper Paperbacks.

Hammer, M. R. 2009. "The Intercultural Development Inventory: An Approach for Assessing and Building Intercultural Competence." In M. A. Moodian (Ed.), *Contemporary Leadership and Intercultural Competence: Exploring the Cross-Cultural Dynamics Within Organizations* (pp. 203–217). Thousand Oaks, CA: Sage Publications.

Hanson, R. 2011. *Just One Thing: Developing a Buddha Brain One Simple Practice at a Time.* Oakland, CA: New Harbinger Publishing.

Hanson, R., and Mendius, R. 2009. *Buddha's Brain: The Practical Neuroscience of Happiness, Love & Wisdom.* Oakland, CA: New Harbinger Publications.

Hyun, J., and Lee, A. S. 2014. *Flex: The New Playbook for Managing Across Difference.* New York: HarperCollins.

Irving, D. 2014. *Waking Up White, and Finding Myself in the Story of Race.* Cambridge, MA: Elephant Room Press.

Johnson, P., and Indvik, J. 1999. "Organizational Benefits of Having Emotionally Intelligent Managers and Employees." *Journal of Workplace Learning*, vol. 11, no. 3, 84–88. doi.org/10.1108/13665629910264226.

Kabat-Zinn, J. 2012. *Mindfulness for Beginners: Reclaiming the Present Moment—and Your Life.* Boulder, CO: Sounds True.

Kang, J., and Lane, K. 2010. "Seeing through Colorblindness: Implicit Bias and the Law." *UCLA Law Review*, vol. 58, 465. UCLA School of Law Research Paper No. 10–22.

Lieberman, M. 2003. "Reflexive and Reflective Judgment Processes: A Social Cognitive Neuroscience Approach." In J. P. Forgas, K. D. Williams, and W. von Hippel (Eds.), *Social Judgments: Implicit and Explicit* Processes (pp. 44–67). New York: Cambridge University Press.

Maak, T., and Pless, N. M. 2009. "Business Leaders as Citizens of the World: Advancing Humanism on a Global Scale." *Journal of Business Ethics*, vol. 88, 537. doi:10.1007/s10551009–0122–0.

Mantzoukas, S. 2005. "The Inclusion of Bias in Reflective and Reflexive Research." *Journal of Research in Nursing*, vol. 10, no. 3, 279–295. doi:10.1177/174498710501000305.

McDonald, K. 2013. *Crafting the Customer Experience for People Not Like You: How to Delight and Engage the Customers Your Competitors Don't Understand.* Hoboken, NJ: John Wiley & Sons.

McNamee, S. J., and Miller, R. K. 2009. *The Meritocracy Myth.* Lanham, MD: Rowman & Littlefield Publishers.

Milgram, S. 1974. *Obedience to Authority: An Experimental View.* New York: HarperCollins.

Mor Barak, M. E. 2011. *Managing Diversity: Toward a Globally Inclusive Workplace.* Thousand Oaks, CA: Sage Publications.

Moss-Racusina, C., Dovidiob, J., et al. 2012. "Science Faculty's Subtle Gender Biases Favor Male Students." *PNAS*, vol. 109, no. 41, 16395–16396.

North, A. C., Hargreaves, D. J., and McKendrick, J. 1999. "The Influence of In-Store Music on Wine Selections." *Journal of Applied Psychology*, vol. 84, no. 2, 271–276.

Nosek, B. A., Smyth, F. L., Hansen, J. J., Devos, T., Lindner, N. M., Ranganath, K. A., and Banaji, M. R. 2007. "Pervasiveness

and Correlates of Implicit Attitudes and Stereotypes." *European Review of Social Psychology*, vol. 18, no. 1, 1–53.

O'Neil, C. 2016. *Weapons of Math Destruction: How Big Data Increases Inequality and Threatens Democracy*. New York: Crown Publishing.

Page, S. E. 2007. *The Difference: How the Power of Diversity Creates Better Groups, Firms, Schools, and Societies*. Princeton, NJ: Princeton University Press.

Patwell, B., and Whitfield Seashore, E. 2006. *Triple Impact Coaching: Use-of-Self in the Coaching Process*. Columbia, MD: Bingham House Books.

Paul, R., and Elder, L. 2016. *The Miniature Guide to Critical Thinking Concepts and Tools*, 7th ed. Tomales, CA: Foundation for Critical Thinking.

Pfister, H., and Bohm, G. 2008. "The Multiplicity of Emotions: A Framework of Emotional Functions in Decision Making." *Judgment and Decision Making*, vol. 3, no. 1, 5–17.

Reeves, A. N. 2015. "Some Uncomfortable Truths." *Chicago Lawyer*, May. nextions.com/wp-content/uploads/2017/05/dip-some-uncomfortable-truths-chicago-lawyer.pdf.

Rivera, L. A. 2015. *Pedigree: How Elite Students Get Elite Jobs*. Princeton, NJ: Princeton University Press.

Robbins, S. L. 2009. *What If? Short Stories to Spark Diversity Dialogue*. Boston: Nicholas Brealey Publishing.

Rothstein, R., and Santow, M. 2012. "A Different Kind of Choice: Educational Inequality and the Continuing Significance of Racial Segregation." Working Paper, Economic Policy Institute, Washington, DC.

Seashore, C. N., Whitfield Seashore, E., and Weinberg, G. M. 2007. *What Did You Say? The Art of Giving and Receiving Feedback.* Columbia, MD: Bingham House Books.

Schein, E. H. 1992. *Organizational Culture and Leadership.* San Francisco: Jossey-Bass Publishers.

Schilt, K. 2011. *Just One of the Guys? Transgender Men and the Persistence of Gender Inequality.* Chicago: University of Chicago Press.

Schmidt, E., and Rosenberg, J. 2014. *How Google Works.* New York: Grand Central Publishing.

Schumacher-Hodge, M. 2016a. "My White Boss Talked About Race in America and This Is What Happened." *Medium*, July 11. medium.com/@MandelaSH/my-white-boss-talked-about-race-in-america-and-this-is-what-happened-fe-10f1a00726#.4zdp8wwc6.

Schumacher-Hodge, M. 2016b. "Dear America: Meet My White Boss That Talks About Race." *Medium*, July 19. medium.com/projectinclude/dear-americameet-my-white-boss-that-talks-about-race-aaa55cd6e780#.4klekjmrt.

Siegel, D. 2010. *Mindsight: The New Science of Personal Transformation.* New York: Random House.

Stanovich, K. 2010. *Rationality & the Reflective Mind.* New York: Oxford University Press.

Steele, C. M. 2010. *Whistling Vivaldi: How Stereotypes Affect Us and What We Can Do.* New York: W. W. Norton & Company.

Steinpreis, R. E., Anders, K. A., and Ritzke, D. 1999. "The Impact of Gender on the Review of Curricula Vitae of Job

Applicants and Tenure Candidates: A National Empirical Study." *Sex Roles*, vol. 41, no. 7–8, 509–28.

Sternberg, R. J. 1997. *Successful Intelligence: How Practical and Creative Intelligence Determine Success in Life*. New York: Plume Publishing.

Storti, C. 1999. *Figuring Foreigners Out: A Practical Guide*. Boston: Intercultural Press.

Tannen, D. 2007. *You Just Don't Understand: Women and Men in Conversation*. New York: William Morrow Publishers.

Vogel, N. O. 2009. *Dive In: Springboard into the Profitability, Productivity, and Potential of the Special Needs Workforce*. Ithaca, NY: Paramount Market Publishing.

Winters, M. F. 2017. *We Can't Talk about That at Work! How to Talk about Race, Religion, Politics, and Other Polarizing Topics*. Oakland, CA: Berrett-Koehler Publishers.

World Economic Forum. 2013. *Human Capital Report*. reports. weforum.org/.

World Economic Forum. 2015. *Global Gender Gap Report*. reports.weforum.org/.

Yaeger, T. F., Head, T. C., and Sorensen, P. F. 2006. *Global Organization Development: Managing Unprecedented Change*. Greenwich, CT: Information Age Publishing.

Yoshino, K. 2007. *Covering*. New York: Random House.

Zander, R. S., and Zander, B. 2002. *The Art of Possibility*. New York: Penguin Group.

Notes

Want to learn more? Take a look at the links and information below to read articles in their entirety, see the research, find the sources, and discover helpful resources.

Introduction

1   Here are the full articles:

www.aol.com/article/finance/2017/02/09/why-hiring-from-all
-walks-of-life-is-the-key-to-success/21711089/.

www.theguardian.com/careers/2017/feb/10
/everybody-wins-when-employers-embrace-diversity.

www.rnews.co.za/article/12974
/diversity-leadership-the-accelerated-quest-for-corporate-winners.

ndsuspectrum.com/diversity-dialogues/.

www.information-age.com
/business-diversity-diverse-workforce-makes-money-123464193/.

2   www.catalyst.org/media/companies-more-women-board-direc-tors-experience-higher-financial-performance-according-latest.

3   www.mckinsey.com/business-functions/organization/our-insights
/why-diversity-matters.

4   Here are some other findings:

McKinsey's 2016 Global Institute Report estimated that improved gender diversity alone could add $12 trillion to the global GDP; www.mckinsey.com/mgi/overview.

Companies with higher percentages of women in management roles also have increasingly higher financial returns. The more women in management, the greater the returns; tribunafeminista.org/wordpress/wp-content/uploads/2016/09/csri_gender_3000.pdf.

The global financial services company Credit-Suisse conducted a study called Gender 3000, showing that companies with at least one woman on the board of directors (BOD) increased return on equity (ROE) by 26% and increased the price-to-book value by 33%; publications.credit-suisse.com/tasks/render/file/index.cfm?fileid=5A7755E1-EFDD-1973-A0B5C54AFF3FB0AE.

5   At the time of this writing, these were the 2017 *DiversityInc* Top 50 Companies for Diversity: www.diversityinc.com /the-diversityinc-top-50-companies-for-diversity-2016/.

6   Grant Thornton International Business Report. 2013. *Women in Senior Management: Setting the Stage for Growth.*

7   womenintheworkplace.com/.

8   In case you'd like to read this fascinating book: Schilt, K. 2011. *Just One of the Guys? Transgender Men and the Persistence of Gender Inequality.* Chicago: University of Chicago Press. To add to the discussion, the World Economic Forum's Global Gender Gap Report ranks countries on four areas that reflect critical themes necessary for women's growth and assigns an overall score. The areas include economic participation and opportunity; educational attainment; health and survival; and political empowerment. Rwanda, Nicaragua, Burundi, Latvia, and twenty-three other countries scored higher than the United States in overall rankings. This is from the World Economic Forum, *The Global Gender Gap Report,* 2015.

9   www.npr.org/2014/07/28/335288388/when-did-companies-become-people-excavating-the-legal-evolution.

10 Johnson, P., and Indvik, J. 1999. "Organizational Benefits of Having Emotionally Intelligent Managers and Employees." *Journal of Workplace Learning,* vol. 11, no. 3, 84–88. doi.org/10.1108/13665629910264226.

11 Salesforce Research. 2017. *Special Report: The Impact of Equality and Values Driven Business,* January. Here's a link also: www.salesforce.com/research/.

Chapter One

1   www.naics.com/counts-by-company-size/.

2   www.talentinnovation.org/publication.cfm?publication=1420.

3   Nosek, B. A., Smyth, F. L., et al. 2007. "Pervasiveness and Correlates of Implicit Attitudes and Stereotypes." *European Review of Social Psychology,* vol. 18, no. 1, 1–53.

4   Ibid.

5   Nosek, B. A., Banaji, M. R., et al. 2002. "Harvesting Implicit Group Attitudes and Beliefs from a Demonstration Website." *Group Dynamics,* vol. 6, no. 1, 101–115.

6   Seaman, J., Beightol, J., et al. 2010. "Contact Theory as a Framework for Experiential Activities as Diversity Education: An Exploratory Study." *Journal of Experiential Education,* vol. 32, no. 3 (May), 207–225.

7   Pettigrew, T. F., and Tropp, L. R. 2008. "How Does Intergroup Contact Reduce Prejudice? Meta-Analytic Tests of Three Mediators." *European Journal of Social Psychology,* vol. 38, 922–934.

8   www.apple.com/support/assets/docs/products/watch/Restricted_Chemicals_for_Wearables.pdf.

9   Blankenship, K., Bray, S., and Merson, M. 2000. "Structural Interventions in Public Health." *AIDS 2000,* vol. 14, Suppl. 1, S11–S21.

10 North, A., Hargreaves, D., and McKendrick, J. 1999. "The Influence of In-Store Music on Wine Selections." *Journal of Applied Psychology,* vol. 84, no. 2, 271–276.

11 Page, S. E. 2007. *The Difference: How the Power of Diversity Creates Better Groups, Firms, Schools, and Societies.* Princeton, NJ: Princeton University Press.

12 Phelps, E. A. 2006. "Emotion and Cognition: Insights from Studies on the Human Amygdala." *Annual Review of Psychology*, vol. 57, 27–53.

13 Brizendine, L. 2006. *The Female Brain*. New York: Broadway Books, p. xiii.

Chapter Two

1   Schein, E. 1992. *Organizational Culture and Leadership*. San Francisco: Jossey-Bass Publishers.

2   www.kaiserpermanentehistory.org.

3   Schein, *Organizational Culture and Leadership*.

4   This chart is adapted from Visions, Inc.

5   SHIFT HR Compliance Training. 2017. "Unconscious Bias: Everything Employers Want to Know." shiftelt.com/wp-content/uploads/2017/04/SHIFT-Unconscious-Bias-White-Pape.pdf.

6   Steinpreis, R. E., Anders, K. A., and Ritzke, D. 1999. "The Impact of Gender on the Review of Curricula Vitae of Job Applicants and Tenure Candidates: A National Empirical Study." *Sex Roles*, vol. 41, no. 7–8, 509–528.

7   Paul, R., and Elder, L. 2016. *The Miniature Guide to Critical Thinking Concepts and Tools*, 7th ed. Tomales, CA: Foundation for Critical Thinking.

8   Berkun, S. 2011. *Mindfire: Big Ideas for Curious Minds*. Seattle: Berkun Media.

9   Ibid.

10 Ibid.

11 theemotionmachine.com.

12 Lieberman, M. 2003. "Reflexive and Reflective Judgment Processes: A Social Cognitive Neuroscience Approach." In J. P. Forgas, K. D. Williams, and W. von Hippel (Eds.), *Social Judgments:*

Implicit and Explicit Processes (pp. 44–67). New York: Cambridge University Press.

13 Siegel, D. 2010. *Mindsight: The New Science of Personal Transformation*. New York: Bantam Books.

14 Kabat-Zinn, J. 2012. *Mindfulness for Beginners: Reclaiming the Present Moment—and Your Life*. Boulder, CO: Sounds True.

15 Tan, C. M. 2012. *Search Inside Yourself: The Unexpected Path to Achieving Profits, Happiness (and World Peace)*. New York: HarperCollins.

16 www.people.fas.harvard.edu/~banaji/.

17 www.tolerance.org/supplement/
strategies-reducing-racial-and-ethnic-prejudice-essential-pr.

18 Moss-Racusina, C., Dovidiob, J., et al. 2012. "Science Faculty's Subtle Gender Biases Favor Male Students." *PNAS*, vol. 109, no. 41, 16395–16296.

19 www.un.org/esa/population/publications/worldaging10502050
/pdf/80chapterii.pdf.

20 Irving, D. 2014. *Waking Up White, and Finding Myself in the Story of Race*. Cambridge, MA: Elephant Room Press.

21 Rothstein, R., and Santow, M. 2012. "A Different Kind of Choice: Educational Inequity and the Continuing Significance of Racial Segregation." Working Paper, Economic Policy Institute, August 21.

22 Irving, *Waking Up White*.

23 McNamee, S. J., and Miller, R. K. 2009. *The Meritocracy Myth*. Lanham, MD: Rowman & Littlefield, pp. 211–216.

24 Tolson, J. 2015. Personal correspondence, July 30.

Chapter Three

1   In the 2015 Economic Report of the President, which examines the US recovery from the Great Recession, it was noted that US

workers' receipt of employer-sponsored training and education has been in decline since 1990 and precipitously dropped 42% between 1996 and 2008: www.nber.org/links/cea_2015_erp.pdf.

2   The Computing Research Association's Taulbee Survey, which documents higher education trends in computer science, computer engineering, and information degree production, shows an astounding six-year consecutive growth trend in undergraduate computing majors, with a 29.2% rise in the 2011–2012 timeframe alone. Overall, PhD production in computing programs reached a record high, with 1,929 degrees granted. The number of both women and minorities in these programs is substantial, with 2,078 degrees awarded to women and 4,127 to minorities in the 2012 survey alone. See Computing Degree and Enrollment Trends, Taulbee Survey, 2011–2012, cra.org.

3   www.hbcu.com.

4   Sternberg, R. J. 1997. *Successful Intelligence: How Practical and Creative Intelligence Determine Success in Life.* New York: Plume Publishing.

5   Rivera, L. A. 2015. *Pedigree: How Elite Students Get Elite Jobs.* Princeton, NJ: Princeton University Press.

6   www.randalolson.com/2014/04/29/u-s-racial-diversity-by-county/.

7   Gould, S. J. 1996. *The Mismeasure of Man*, rev. ed. New York: W. W. Norton & Company.

8   Kang, J., and Lane, K. 2010. "Seeing Through Colorblindness: Implicit Bias and the Law." *UCLA Law Review*, vol. 58, June 30, 465. UCLA School of Law Research Paper No. 10–22.

9   Banaji, M. R., and Greenwald, A. G. 2013. *Blindspot: Hidden Biases of Good People.* New York: Delacourt Press, p. 147.

10 Davies, A., Fidler, D., and Gorbis, M. 2011. *Future Work Skills 2020.* Institute for the Future: University of Phoenix Research Institute, Palo Alto, CA. www.iftf.org.

11 www.payscale.com. Note that this data reflects 2013, the most recent available at the time of this writing.

12 Gabriel, S., and Gardner, W. L. 1999. "Are There 'His' and 'Hers' Types of Interdependence? The Implications of Gender Differences in Collective versus Relational Interdependence for Affect, Behavior, and Cognition." *Journal of Personality and Social Psychology*, vol. 77, no. 3 (September), 642–655. dx.doi.org/10.1037/0022-3514.77.3.642.

13 Paustian-Underdahl, S. C., Walker, L. S., and Woehr, D. J. 2014. "Gender and Perceptions of Leadership Effectiveness: A Meta-Analysis of Contextual Moderators." *Journal of Applied Psychology*, vol. 99, no. 6, 1129–11145.

14 Rivers, C., and Barnett, R. C. 2015. *The New Soft War on Women*. New York: TarcherPerigee/Penguin.

15 ourplace.co/myth-busted-older-workers-just-tech-savvy-younger-ones-says-new-survey/.

16 Buckingham, M., and Goodall, A. 2015. "Reinventing Performance Management." *Harvard Business Review*, April.

17 www.catalyst.org/zing/how-new-discrimination-holding-women-back.

18 womenintheworkplace.com/.

19 www.pewresearch.org/fact-tank/2016/07/01/racial-gender-wage-gaps-persist-in-u-s-despite-some-progress/.

20 Seashore, C., Whitfield Seashore, E., and Weinberg, G. 1992. *What Did You Say? The Art of Giving and Receiving Feedback*. Columbia, MD: Bingham House Books.

21 Patwell, B., and Whitfield Seashore, E. 2010. *Triple Impact Coaching: Use-of-Self in the Coaching Process*, 2nd ed. Columbia, MD: Bingham House Books.

22 Maak, T., and Pless, N. M. 2009. "Business Leaders as Citizens of the World. Advancing Humanism on a Global Scale." *Journal of Business Ethics*, vol. 88, 537. doi:10.1007/s10551-009-0122-0.

23 Jensen, M. 2007. *12 Inclusive Behaviors*. The Kaleel Jamison Consulting Group, Inc.

24 Milgram, S. 1974. *Obedience to Authority: An Experimental View.*
    New York: HarperCollins.

25 Detert, J. R., and Edmondson, A. C. 2011. "Implicit Voice The-
    ories: Taken-for-Granted Rules of Self-Censorship at Work."
    Academy of Management Journal, vol. 54, 461–476.

Chapter Four

1 Ferdman, B. M., Deane, B. R., et al. 2014. *Diversity at Work: The
   Practice of Inclusion.* San Francisco: Jossey-Bass Publishers, p. 3.

2 Ibid.

3 Reeves, A. N. 2015. "Some Uncomfortable Truths." *Chicago
   Lawyer*, May. nextions.com/wp-content/uploads/2017/05
   /dip-some-uncomfortable-truths-chicago-lawyer.pdf.

4 www.theguardian.com/us-news/2017/aug/14/
   kenneth-frazier-quits-trump-business-panel.

5 www.diversityinc.com/featured-partners/kaiser-permanen-
   te-ceo-bernard-tyson-racism-discrimination-cannot-tolerated/.

6 Schumacher-Hodge, M. 2016. "My White Boss Talked About
   Race in America and This Is What Happened." *Medium*, July 11.
   medium.com/@MandelaSH/my-white-boss-talked-about-race-in-
   america-and-this-is-what-happened-fe10f1a00726#.4zdp8wwc6.

7 Schumacher-Hodge, M. 2016. "Dear America: Meet My White
   Boss That Talks About Race." *Medium*, July 19. medium.com/pro-
   jectinclude/dear-america-meet-my-white-boss-that-talks-about-
   race-aaa55cd6e780#.4klekjmrt.

8 www.businessinsider.com/diversity-initiative-ceos-2017-6.

9 Winters, M. F. 2017. *We Can't Talk about That at Work! How to Talk
   about Race, Religion, Politics, and Other Polarizing Topics.* Oakland,
   CA: Berrett-Koehler Publishers.

10 idiinventory.com/products/
    the-intercultural-development-inventory-idi/

11 Hammer, M. R. 2009. "The Intercultural Development Inventory:
    An Approach for Assessing and Building Intercultural Compe-
    tence." In M. A. Moodian (Ed.), *Contemporary Leadership and
    Intercultural Competence: Exploring the Cross-Cultural Dynamics
    Within Organizations* (pp. 203–217). Thousand Oaks, CA:
    Sage Publications.

12 www.kilmanndiagnostics.com/
    overview-thomas-kilmann-conflict-mode-instrument-tki.

13 Ibid. Page 8.

Chapter Five

1   Balter, R., Chow, J., and Jin, Y. 2014. "What Diversity Metrics Are
    Best Used to Track and Improve Employee Diversity?" Cornell Uni-
    versity, ILR School site, digitalcommons.ilr.cornell/edu/student/68.

2   Yamkovenko, B., and Tavares, S. 2017. "To Understand Whether
    Your Company Is Inclusive, Map How Your Employees Interact."
    Harvard Business Review, July 19.

3   Ibid.

Conclusion: Bringing It All Together

1   Gates, W. H. III. 1999. *Business @ the Speed of Thought.* New York:
    Warner Books.

2   www.ceoaction.com/the-pledge/.

Appendix One

1   O'Neil, C. 2016. *Weapons of Math Destruction: How Big Data
    Increases Inequality and Threatens Democracy.* New York: Crown
    Publishing.

Index

global female workforce representation, 18
innovative approaches to identifying needed talent, 101
intervention in behalf of other
groups, 62, 120
lack of progress in diversity, 6–8
male adaptations by women, 119
pay gap metrics, 183, 186–87
performance evaluation systems, 125
preventing interviewer bias, 107
questioning assumptions, 74
ranking of countries on themes
necessary for women's
growth, 218
stereotypes regarding emotion,
41
unconscious bias, 25–26, 63, 78
valuing women, 119–21
virtual and augmented reality,
123
women in STEM positions, 19
women in symphony orches-
tras, 107
Gender 3000 (Credit-Suisse), 218
General Electric, 126
"G" (general measure of intelligence), 105
GI Bill, 84
Girls Teaching Girls to Code, 101
Girls Who Code, 101
"glass ceiling," 7
Global Gender Gap Report
(World Economic Forum), 218
Global Institute Report (McK-
insey & Company), 217
Google, 5–7, 33, 71, 99
average tenure, 117
success though non-diverse, 202
Google Ventures, 96

Gorbis, Marina, 205
Grace Hopper Celebration, 101
Gray, John, 46

H
Hall, Edward T., 53
Handler, Barbara, 100
Handler, Ruth, 100
Harvard Business Review, 179
Harvard University, 21, 100
HBCUs (historically Black colleges and universities), 99
healthcare industry, 109–10
hidden bias. *See* unconscious bias
Highly Reliable Surgical Teams
(HRSTs), 33–34
"high-potential" (hi-po) model,
127, 194
Hire America's Heroes, 101
hiring process, 106–17. *See also*
employee retention and
engagement; talent search
appreciative inquiry, 113–14, 193
bar against which candidates
are measured, 114–15, 193
behavioral-based interview
questions, 111–12
bias in interview process, 106–8
critical skills needed in environments of rapid change,
115–16, 205–6
hard and soft skills, 115–17
"hiring for nice," 109
holistic hiring, 109–11, 193
interviewer bias, 106–8, 193
predictive analytics tools, 108
reshaping thinking about,
112–17
subjective nature of, 106, 114
historically Black colleges and
universities (HBCUs), 99

About the Author

Barbara Adams is Founder and Chief Learning Officer at GAR (Gender, Age, and Race) Diversity Consulting, based in the San Francisco Bay Area. She holds a Doctorate of Psychology in Organizational Development. Dr. Adams is a former director in the National Diversity & Inclusion office at Kaiser Permanente (KP), the largest nonprofit, integrated healthcare system in the United States, consistently ranked among the top performers in the *DiversityInc* Top 50 annual survey. Before KP, Dr. Adams spent a decade in global management and technology consulting with American Management Systems (now CGI). She can be reached at drbarbadams.com.

PERMISSIONS CREDITS (CONTINUED)